DARE TO BE DIVINE

A journey into the miraculous

Richard Rudd

GENE KEYS

First edition published in Great Britain and USA 2021
by Gene Keys Publishing Ltd
13 Freeland Park, Wareham Road
Poole BH16 6FA

Copyright © Richard Rudd 2017, 2021, 2023

All rights reserved. No part of this book may be reproduced or utilised in any form or by any means, electronic or mechanical, without prior permission in writing from the publishers.

Richard Rudd

DARE TO BE DIVINE
A journey into the miraculous

Hardback Book Edition ISBN: 978-1-9996710-9-9
Kindle Edition ISBN: 978-1-913820-08-4

Transcribed and edited by Richard Rudd and Danne Saring.
Dare to be Divine logo design by Danne Saring.

The content in this book and/or course is purely inspirational which you may choose to use on a personal journey of investigation and exploration. This should not be entered into lightly. It is to be used with the understanding that neither the publisher nor author is engaged to render any type of psychological or other professional advice in any way, shape or form. The content of the book and/or course is the sole expression and opinion of its author, and not necessarily that of the publisher. No warranties or guarantees are expressed or implied. The publishers take no responsibly for how you use the content.

genekeys.com

ABOUT THE AUTHOR

Richard Rudd is an international teacher, writer, and award-winning poet. His mystical journey began early in life when he experienced a life-changing state of spiritual illumination over 3 days and nights in his twenties. This catalysed an extensive worldwide spiritual search. All his studies became synthesised in 2002 when he began to write and receive the Gene Keys, a vast synthesis exploring the miraculous possibilities inherent in human DNA. It took seven years to write the book as well as understand and embody its teachings. Today Richard continues to study and teach the profound lessons contained in the Gene Keys.

TABLE OF CONTENTS

INTRODUCTION	1
ORIENTATION	19
PART ONE — THE FIRST FOUR DARES **THE SACRED LETTERS OF LIGHT**	29

The First Dare — Dare to See the Beauty in Everything — 33

The 1st Siddhi - Beauty - Beauty is Always New — 33

The 28th Siddhi - Immortality - Beauty is Forever — 36

The 43rd Siddhi - Epiphany - True Beauty Lies Within — 37

The 44th Siddhi - Synarchy - Beauty Cannot Exist in Isolation — 38

The Second Dare — Dare to Be the One — 41

The 2nd Siddhi - Unity - Our Unfallen State — 41

The 23rd Siddhi - Quintessence - Love is the Fifth Element — 43

The 24th Siddhi - Silence - Oneness is a Silent Mind — 44

The 27th Siddhi - Selflessness - The Doctrine of Harmlessness — 45

The Third Dare — Dare to Be Truthful — 49

The 63rd Siddhi - Truth - Absolute Truth is Collective — 50

The 38th Siddhi - Honour - The Eternal Warrior — 51

The 40th Siddhi - Divine Will - Omnipotence in Action — 52

The 54th Siddhi - Ascension - Seek and Ye Shall Find — 53

The Fourth Dare — Dare to Be Illuminated — 57

The 64th Siddhi - Illumination - Light is Limitless — 57

The 39th Siddhi - Liberation - Unlocking the Light in your DNA — 59

The 37th Siddhi - Tenderness - The Light of the World — 60

The 53rd Siddhi - Superabundance - How to Become a Millionaire — 61

PART TWO — THE SECOND FOUR DARES — SOLVE ET COAGULA — 65

THE FIFTH DARE — DARE TO BE DISSOLVED — 71

The 14th Siddhi - Bounteousness - The Dissolution of Power — 72

The 32nd Siddhi - Veneration - Jacob's Ladder — 75

The 34th Siddhi - Majesty - The Olympians — 78

The 50th Siddhi - Harmony - Harmony of the Spheres — 79

THE SIXTH DARE — DARE TO SURRENDER — 85

The 3rd Siddhi - Innocence - Surrendering to Change — 87

The 8th Siddhi - Exquisiteness - Surrendering your Self-Image — 89

The 20th Siddhi - Presence - Surrendering to the Now — 91

The 42nd Siddhi - Celebration - Surrendering to Death — 93

THE SEVENTH DARE — DARE TO BE DECISIVE — 99

The 15th Siddhi - Florescence - Love Thy Neighbour as Thyself — 102

The 22nd Siddhi - Grace - The Descent of the Dove — 104

The 36th Siddhi - Compassion - The Dark Night of the Soul — 106

The 52nd Siddhi - Stillness - The Still Point — 109

THE EIGHTH DARE — DARE TO BE GENTLE — 115

The 6th Siddhi - Peace - Peace on Earth and Goodwill — 116

The 10th Siddhi - Being - Sitting by the River — 118

The 47th Siddhi - Transfiguration - Karmic Supernova — 121

The 58th Siddhi - Bliss - Blessed are the Meek — 124

PART THREE — THE THIRD FOUR DARES — THE COMING OF HOMO SANCTUS — 129

The Ninth Dare — Dare to Be Immortal — 135

The 30th Siddhi - Rapture - The Blade of Rapture — 137

The 55th Siddhi - Freedom - The Blade of Freedom — 138

The 56th Siddhi - Intoxication - The Blade of Intoxication — 139

The 62nd Siddhi - Impeccability - The Blade of Impeccability — 141

The Tenth Dare — Dare to Care — 145

The 29th Siddhi - Devotion - Bhakti Yoga — 148

The 59th Siddhi - Transparency - Open for Business — 149

The 60th Siddhi - Justice - Judgement Day — 151

The 61st Siddhi - Sanctity - The Holy of Holies — 152

The Eleventh Dare — Dare to Be a Warrior — 155

The 5th Siddhi - Timelessness - Breaking Bad Habits — 156

The 9th Siddhi - Invincibility - Love is in the Detail — 157

The 48th Siddhi - Wisdom - Acting from No Mind — 159

The 57th Siddhi - Clarity - Knowing the Future — 160

The Twelfth Dare — Dare to Break Free — 163

The 16th Siddhi - Mastery - If Not Now, When? — 165

The 21st Siddhi - Valour - If Not You, Who? — 166

The 35th Siddhi - Boundlessness - Catching the Miraculous Wind — 168

The 51st Siddhi - Awakening - Leaping the Moat — 169

PART FOUR — THE FINAL FOUR DARES EARTH ASCENDING	**173**
THE THIRTEENTH DARE — DARE TO BE CHOSEN	**179**
The 13th Siddhi - Empathy - Fractal Relationships	180
The 31st Siddhi - Humility - The Round Table	181
The 33st Siddhi - Revelation - Total Recall	183
The 49th Siddhi - Rebirth - The New World Order	186
THE FOURTEENTH DARE — DARE TO BE SILENT	**191**
The 4th Siddhi - Forgiveness - Returning Non-Love with Love	192
The 7th Siddhi - Virtue - An Army of Virtues	193
The 19th Siddhi - Sacrifice - The Silent Tsunami	194
The 41st Siddhi - Emanation - The Golden Goose	195
THE FIFTEENTH DARE — DARE TO ASCEND	**199**
The 11th Siddhi - Light - White Magick	200
The 18th Siddhi - Perfection - The Perfect Paradox	201
The 26th Siddhi - Invisibility - The Earth Grid	203
The 46th Siddhi - Ecstasy - Eating Mangoes	204
THE SIXTEENTH DARE — DARE TO BE DIVINE	**209**
The 12th Siddhi - Purity - Heart of a Child	210
The 17th Siddhi - Omniscience - The Eye of the I	211
The 25th Siddhi - Universal Love - The Guild of the Grail	213
The 45th Siddhi - Communion - Union of All Beings	214

The text of this book has been transcribed from the author's original video series. Although slight changes have been made to the text, we have endeavoured to retain the informal flow, style and cadence of the original oral transmission.

To get the most out of this teaching, we recommend you also purchase the full *Dare to Be Divine* online course, which contains the original audio/visual transmission, available from our shop on **genekeys.com**

PREFACE

My name is Richard Rudd and I am the founder of a wisdom called the Gene Keys. People often ask me, 'Well what are the Gene Keys?' I don't really have a predefined answer to this question. There are as many responses to that question as there are human beings. However, for the record, the Gene Keys are a synthesis based on a multidimensioned approach that brings together science, art, mysticism, the social sciences, mythology, music, and just about any other subject that you can name. You might ask here: how can I possibly claim to synthesise all these things?

The answer is that the Gene Keys are based on a universal code representing all life. That code has its root in the Chinese I Ching, an ancient book written over 5,000 years ago. When you can read and understand this code, you have at your fingertips an extraordinary system of timeless wisdom.

The Gene Keys may be used both as a practical wisdom and as a deep contemplative tool to expand your consciousness. Above all, the Gene Keys gives you a vision of yourself and your life, far beyond what you might ever have considered possible. Our modern, materialistic world has lost touch with the magical roots of the cosmos; we tend to see life through the logical scientific brain. That is fascinating, revealing, and useful, but it is also essentially limiting. Logic itself is self-limiting. Logic for example can never fully grasp a concept like infinity. Since logic is based on cause and effect, how can it understand a concept such as infinity which is beyond cause and effect?

You know, you're always going to hit the same paradox. When they were young my kids always asked me the question that all parents know: 'What was before the beginning of the universe?' and whatever logical answer I would try to give them, they would always come back to me with that same response: 'But Daddy, what was before that?'

Logic is limited by its logicality and therefore it cannot penetrate the veils of the deep mystery. In *Dare to be Divine*, I shall try to present something to you that is *alogical* – it is beyond logic. In other words, where we are going, logic breaks down.

The ancients called this world we live in, a *maya* – an illusion fabricated by the mind. Truth, they also say, is something that can only be known by direct experience; never by mere thinking or reasoning. How can the mind understand the illusion, since in itself it is an instrument *of* the illusion?

To engage fully with this material, you will therefore need to step beyond the mind. I have no scientific credentials, so if you're looking for scientific verification of this wisdom, all I can say is that material science hasn't caught up yet, and maybe it never will.

However, I do have one thing that does give me a bit of an edge – in my early twenties, I had a direct experience of truth – Truth with a capital T. The experience I had was so vast it can't be comprehended by the everyday conditioned mind. I perceived the unity of all things. I was living a quiet contemplative life, and one morning I woke up and everything was just different. I am unable to fully explain or put into words what I experienced, but for several days my body was flooded with light. It emanated and radiated from every pore of my being.

This light was not physical light. It was not like the light that we see. This light carried intelligence. It was alive and it connected me to everything. It shone through my mind like crystal. Anything I wanted to know, I could instantly know. From the past, from the future, I saw everything all at once in a great sweep. I felt I was being seen through because I, Richard Rudd, was no more in that space. There was just the presence, this eternal presence beyond time and beyond space.

This lifequake lasted three days and three nights. Neither did I sleep. There was no sleep in that world, and it shook me to the roots of my being. It redefined my life and has reshaped my decisions and my destiny from that time on.

I was prepared to live a so-called ordinary life. Instead, I became a seeker of Truth and later also a teacher of Truth. Having tasted the beyond, I wanted more. Today, twenty years later, my search has led me all over the world. It has led me to teachers and teachings from the ancient world to those of contemporary times.

Then, at a precise moment in my journey, when I was ready, a huge book came through me. I called it *The Gene Keys, Embracing your Higher Purpose*. It took me seven years to write and in its pages, I encapsulate in coded form, everything that happened to me, more or less, in those three days back in the early nineties.

A JOURNEY INTO THE MIRACULOUS

As the name suggests, the Gene Keys are a code that corresponds to your DNA. This correlation occurs through the 64-fold mathematics of the code. The light of consciousness that I experienced (and that others have also experienced), came from within the cellular and genetic structure of who I am. However, since I am no scientist, the Gene Keys are a poet's exploration of human DNA. They are a mystic exploration of the full and unrealised potential hidden in the 64 codons that make up our genetic code.

As I continued to explore the grand synthesis of the Gene Keys in the years following my experience, I began to realise that we humans have access to a whole spectrum of consciousness. In other words, there are dimensions available to us that lie beyond the physical senses. In fact, we are headed as a species towards our very highest potential.

Normally our notion of potential, concerns how successful we can be in the outer world – to find love, to be wealthy, to do well materially and emotionally; to be happy and prosperous. But this teaching will travel far beyond those concepts. We shall look beyond individual well-being, into the deep mystery of our existence. Following my experience, and over the past twenty years, I have sought out human beings who attained states of consciousness like the one I experienced. I have read about them, I have studied them extensively and I have even met some of them in the flesh.

In my travels, I've heard stories that would make most people put up their blinds. These stories occur in all cultures. They usually revolve around saints or sages rather than around statesmen, scientists, or geniuses. Most of these stories are instantly dismissed by the sceptics with their logical worldview. Miracles are generally relegated to the domain of fantasy or delusion or regarded as quaint perspectives of a more primitive, indigenous culture that we have now evolved beyond.

Those living on the plane of the miraculous, however, are not easy to approach with a logical mind. We have to meet such a person face to face, to receive the palpable presence of the other dimensions. In this book, I will share some of these stories.

Let's begin the journey with such a story:

You might be familiar with this one about the late Ram Dass, a spiritual teacher from America, and his teacher Neem Karoli Baba, nicknamed Maharaji. The story goes that one day, Ram Dass, while enjoying these higher devotional states around his teacher, had to go down into the valley; perhaps to renew his visa. He wore his regalia – his robes and his mala and he was inhabiting this holy higher state. He took lunch in a small place in his full yogi costume. With the vegetarian lunch was a little chocolate biscuit on the side.

He says in his story that this definitely was *not* yogi food, but without anyone in the restaurant seeing, he managed to eat and surreptitiously enjoy the biscuit.

Several weeks later when he had gone back up into the mountains, the very first thing Maharaji said on seeing Ram Dass was: 'So, how did you enjoy the biscuit?'

Small things like this can really open up your mind because our real potential is simply off the map. Our true potential is actually unlimited. For most people that's too much to stomach; science and logic prevail. We feel the deep limitation of our mortality, of our body and the material world and its laws. The irony however, is that even science now suspects strongly that matter itself is porous. It may well be that the presence of other dimensions is the only way to explain the workings of the universe.

So, let us begin here with the concept that your true potential is limitless.

Your ability to open up to this concept is the beginning of a journey into this magical world that lies beyond the senses. If you cannot get past this concept, then you needn't waste your time with this teaching. If, however, even a small part of you can accept that anything is possible, it will open you up to a whole new universe.

There is nothing to understand here in this teaching. This isn't a training. It isn't educational. It isn't clever. You can sit back, relax and enjoy it as though you were watching a movie. But you can also reflect on this movie because you're in it! As you watch, you can see perhaps what kind of role you have been playing and whether that role might change as you expand your notion of who you really are.

Dare to be Divine is like sitting in a jacuzzi of high frequencies. You need only soften, let them in, and contemplate them over time... The rest will take care of itself.

INTRODUCTION

Dare To Be Divine

WELCOME TO DARE TO BE DIVINE

In this teaching, we are going to take an extraordinary journey. I believe this may never have been done before. We are going to journey into the deep matrix of our highest potential, both individually and as a species. We are going to journey far, far back into our ancestral past, to an age where we existed as a more merged being, a more mythical collective consciousness. At the same time, we shall travel far, far forwards into our common future, into the vast unrealised potential we have as human beings, but not only as human beings. We shall travel onwards towards our eventual divinity.

We will be using the Chinese I Ching as the primary roadmap into our infinite divine potential. Traditionally, the I Ching has been used in a practical way to help people understand their current life situation and to support them in making clear decisions so that they can follow the way of harmony.

However, in this teaching, we will be using the I Ching in a new way. It may even have been originally conceived to do this – to see into our future. One might ask why we should gaze into the crystal ball of our future? Won't that take us away from the present and off into a world of daydream and fantasy?

It won't as long as we have a clear understanding. This teaching is a part of the Gene Keys transmission, and if you know anything about the Gene Keys, you'll be aware that they are a very grounded wisdom teaching – rooted in the earth and in everyday life.

So, if you are reading this book or studying the *Dare to be Divine* online programme as your introduction to the Gene Keys, please know that it is designed to go alongside the Gene Keys transmission as a whole, and in particular, *The Golden Path*, whose teaching will ground you into your body, into your humanity, and into your mundane mortality.

You may make use of this wisdom to elevate your spirit, to pull you out of those dark places we all sometimes fall into, and to give you a fresh and beautiful perspective on living, dying, and the purpose of suffering itself. But you are recommended to stay consistent with the core teachings – so that you can bring them to our wonderful earth, our Mother, to show up fully in your life, whatever circumstances are put before you.

We come here with the Gene Keys to learn a new inner language – the language of the codes upon which our entire universe is built. The words of this language are woven of frequencies. These frequencies can elevate our consciousness and increase our self-awareness. It is important, therefore, to become familiar with the language – with the actual words in this spectrum of consciousness. I have spoken and written extensively on all these words for *The Gene Keys, Embracing Your Higher Purpose*, so you can explore them for yourself in depth.

In this teaching, we come to gaze into the words for the 64 Siddhis – the most elevated words in the Gene Keys pantheon. Sometimes I have also called them the *64 Names of Love*. They are the original language of light. If you hear the essence of just a single one of these names, you will be blessed, for you will hear the sacred *Om* at the heart of creation. That is the way that these words can take us beyond the word. They can carry us up into the causal plane, that plane of being where words cease, where we can see the holographic truth of our higher consciousness – where we begin to merge back into the field of light from which we are woven.

This teaching may be a challenge for many of us. It is designed to open us up to higher possibilities and insights. It is designed to help us reach deeper into our humanity and to open our hearts and minds more widely than ever before.

Before launching into hyperspace, we should get grounded in some basics, particularly if you are new to the Gene Keys.

Introduction

The core foundation of the Gene Keys is the *Spectrum of Consciousness*. (See table below). The Spectrum is made up of 64 codes known as the Gene Keys, and each Gene Key is divided into three levels called frequency bands. These bands are described as the Shadow, the Gift, and the Siddhi.

	SHADOW	GIFT	SIDDHI		SHADOW	GIFT	SIDDHI
1	Entropy	Freshness	Beauty	33	Forgetting	Mindfulness	Revelation
2	Dislocation	Orientation	Unity	34	Force	Strength	Majesty
3	Chaos	Innovation	Innocence	35	Hunger	Adventure	Boundlessness
4	Intolerance	Understanding	Forgiveness	36	Turbulence	Humanity	Compassion
5	Impatience	Patience	Timelessness	37	Weakness	Equality	Tenderness
6	Conflict	Diplomacy	Peace	38	Struggle	Perseverance	Honour
7	Division	Guidance	Virtue	39	Provocation	Dynamism	Liberation
8	Mediocrity	Style	Exquisiteness	40	Exhaustion	Resolve	Divine Will
9	Inertia	Determination	Invincibility	41	Fantasy	Anticipation	Emanation
10	Self-Obsession	Naturalness	Being	42	Expectation	Detachment	Celebration
11	Obscurity	Idealism	Light	43	Deafness	Insight	Epiphany
12	Vanity	Discrimination	Purity	44	Interference	Teamwork	Synarchy
13	Discord	Discernment	Empathy	45	Dominance	Synergy	Communion
14	Compromise	Competence	Bounteousness	46	Seriousness	Delight	Ecstasy
15	Dullness	Magnetism	Florescence	47	Oppression	Transmutation	Transfiguration
16	Indifference	Versatility	Mastery	48	Inadequacy	Resourcefulness	Wisdom
17	Opinion	Far-Sightedness	Omniscience	49	Reaction	Revolution	Rebirth
18	Judgement	Integrity	Perfection	50	Corruption	Equilibrium	Harmony
19	Co-Dependence	Sensitivity	Sacrifice	51	Agitation	Initiative	Awakening
20	Superficiality	Self-Assurance	Presence	52	Stress	Restraint	Stillness
21	Control	Authority	Valour	53	Immaturity	Expansion	Superabundance
22	Dishonour	Graciousness	Grace	54	Greed	Aspiration	Ascension
23	Complexity	Simplicity	Quintessence	55	Victimisation	Freedom	Freedom
24	Addiction	Invention	Silence	56	Distraction	Enrichment	Intoxication
25	Constriction	Acceptance	Universal Love	57	Unease	Intuition	Clarity
26	Pride	Artfulness	Invisibility	58	Dissatisfaction	Vitality	Bliss
27	Selfishness	Altruism	Selflessness	59	Dishonesty	Intimacy	Transparency
28	Purposelessness	Totality	Immortality	60	Limitation	Realism	Justice
29	Half-Heartedness	Commitment	Devotion	61	Psychosis	Inspiration	Sanctity
30	Desire	Lightness	Rapture	62	Intellect	Precision	Impeccability
31	Arrogance	Leadership	Humility	63	Doubt	Inquiry	Truth
32	Failure	Preservation	Veneration	64	Confusion	Imagination	Illumination

THE SPECTRUM OF CONSCIOUSNESS
Shadow, Gift and Siddhi

If you look down the Shadow frequency band above, you can see that these words are all human states that cause misery and suffering – conflict, corruption, unease, stress, intolerance, and so on. These are the psychological victim patterns that catch us in their claws and can literally hijack an entire life.

All the shadow states are fear states. They are part of the ancient reptilian programming from the older parts of our brain. However, we have a choice with how we use those parts of our brain and indeed, whether we use them or not.

One significant revelation emerging from deep contemplation of this spectrum is that fear is a choice. Each of these states represents a frequency band, and like a radio set, we can attune ourselves to them. If for example you watch the news on TV every day and you believe this is all the world is, you are programming deep into your being, into your DNA, a worldview that is generally based on fear. When you listen to the words used in the headlines, you will hear these kinds of shadow words being repeated more than any other type of word. Ask yourself then: how are you programming yourself? That is worthy of deep consideration.

The next level in the spectrum is called the Gift frequency. This is quite beautiful because it touches our genius. Our genius only comes alive when we're willing to confront the shadows. Then those shadows, like butterflies emerging from caterpillars, transform into our gifts. It's the old cliché that every cloud has a silver lining.

Every shadow contains a gift. Maybe there are few true geniuses in the world because genius lies in the last place you would ever think to look. Genius lies in the heart of your actual suffering. You have to embrace your own shadow.

As in the ancient myths, you have to go down into the underworld and free yourself from the old fear patterns and your self-limiting beliefs. When you finally manage to do this, a huge amount of energy and enthusiasm is released. It changes your body, your chemistry, and your whole being. You fill again with vitality – you stop feeling so tired and drained. You become creative, open, and optimistic once again, just as you were when you were a young child.

Only deep acceptance and self-compassion can unlock the potential of our shadow and transform it into our creative genius – the Gift frequency. In the centre of the spectrum, you can see all the words for these gifts laid out like a directory of all human genius. These are human archetypes, types of latent genius waiting to be unlocked. Some examples are the Genius of Commitment, the Genius of Detachment, the Genius of Revolution, and the Genius of Altruism.

Although these appear to be just words, they are in fact keys to a secret door inside us. Behind each one lies a whole world in which we are invited to transform our challenges into opportunities for transmutation and joy.

When you look into each Gene Key you can see how this works. For instance, taking the 12th Gene Key, you'll see that the shadow is called Vanity. This is human narcissism – our tendency to behave as though we are the centre of the universe. But the gift here is Discrimination. As we learn to see through our vanity and self-obsession, we learn to use that insight to help others and thus we become more discriminating.

The highest aspect here, which I call the Siddhi (a Sanskrit word meaning divine gift), is Purity. This is our pure heart. Deep down inside us, we all have the same pure heart, but only through the journey of discrimination can we reach and realise that inner purity. Perhaps you can see here the way vanity and purity are connected at the polar ends of the spectrum.

So, in this sense, it isn't really a spectrum! The purity is hidden within the vanity. The Shadow contains the Gift and the Siddhi. The higher, hidden purpose of our suffering is therefore to take us up to our highest potential.

From the shadow to the gift is a great leap in consciousness. A person living in their shadows doesn't truly believe that anything is possible. Their life seems a dead-end street. They feel trapped, tired, and ground down by the relentless struggle of mundane life. They are exhausted by their relationships and the futile search for stability, wealth, and health – we all know the story.

But a person living out their gifts is completely different. They are creative, self-empowered, humble, and joyous; life can't get them down for too long, for they have integrated their unique collection of gifts. They are human but strong in their vulnerability. They are a hub of transformation. Although they suffer like everyone else (and sometimes more) they don't allow their suffering to get the best of them. They use it as fuel, to live their life at a higher level, creating opportunities where before were only problems.

Then, of course, there is one more level, one more quantum leap. This is the icing on the cake. The icing – to pun with the I Ching – is what this teaching is all about: I sing. The icing is the final level of consciousness called the siddhi. I had to turn to this Sanskrit word for want of a word in English. A siddhi is – more or less – a divine gift or a superpower frequency. You know that game where you and your young child, or anyone, ask each other: If you could have any superpower, what would yours be?

Well, the Siddhis are your superpower. You can see in the process of vanity transforming to purity through the Gift of Discrimination, the relationship between the Shadow and the Siddhi, between what gets you down the most and your very highest potential.

THE 64 SIDDHIS – AN ENCYCLOPAEDIA OF ENLIGHTENMENT

These siddhis are not just passing states. They can be stabilised into permanent stages of consciousness. They are fields of frequency, and there are 64 of these siddhic fields. Or you could see them as a single over-arching field with many different variations of one vast pervasive truth. These 64 are all the states of consciousness available to human beings – the latent potential hidden in the 64 codons of our DNA. They require an ultra-high frequency code to unlock them. This is the unlimited you, your higher self, your divinity, your greatest purpose in life.

So what is the code that unlocks such rarefied states and how do we activate it? That is the golden question asked by humans down the aeons. However, before going into this further, I invite you to take some time with the Spectrum of Consciousness, to contemplate it.

Spend some time looking at the states of consciousness. Maybe some of those words will jump out at you. Maybe some of those Shadows seem familiar as well. The Gene Keys are a journey into these codes, and I particularly recommend spending some time considering the siddhis, those extraordinary higher states of consciousness. Open your mind up to the possibility that these are states that you can attain. In the beginning, that's all that's required.

When I was first naming this spectrum of siddhis, I was in something of an expanded state, and for some reason, I put into my Google search engine: 64 siddhis. It was therefore extraordinary to me to find a whole tradition of this from the ancient wisdom teachings of India. There's a verse in the original text of the Vedas that speaks specifically of the 64 siddhis. That blew me away. But further elucidation is not given in the vedas as to what they really are.

Perhaps the Gene Keys are a returning cycle of this original wisdom that was discovered so many thousands of years ago...

For those of you who are new to the Gene Keys, the Gene Keys also provide us with a unique profiling system called your Hologenetic Profile. You can obtain your profile for free on the genekeys.com website. Your profile shows you the specific gene keys which relate to the various areas of your life. In other words, each of us has specific keys out of the total of 64 which dictate various themes and stages in our life. There are gene keys that release prosperity, gene keys that ensure good health, and gene keys that open our hearts and heal our relationships. This whole wisdom is a journey, an adventure into your inner world. If you want to change your outer world, you first of all must change the inside.

The single purpose of this four-part teaching is to dive exclusively into these 64 siddhis. These extraordinary words and states of consciousness can seem far away from everyday life but in fact, they are closer than we realise. It might take a bit of work to get there, but we each have a unique route into this higher wisdom within us.

The Gene Keys provide your specific code and your route into the higher consciousness. In this sense the Gene Keys are unique. There may not have been a knowledge like this for some time in the world – an encyclopaedia of enlightenment, a specific guide to the self-realised state.

The Gene Keys open a pathway of love, wisdom, and truth. This is knowledge that is timeless and ancient, simple and practical, and alive. The wisdom is alive within us. It's not a book or a system, it's not in these words, it is behind all that, it's in us all, it's in you right now as you read these very words. It is immediate and available. You have only to knock on the door.

STATES AND STAGES

How to activate these Siddhis? Let's consider this. *Should* we try and activate higher states? Are there dangers in trying? The ancients often warned us about the higher states, the so-called 'lure of the Siddhis'. We are warned not to seek such things, and there is value in this warning. The ancient masters were talking about seeking miraculous powers for the sake of personal ambition. I want to make it clear that I am talking about something quite different here.

The 64 Siddhis that we are speaking of are not magical powers, although they may lead to miraculous states or manifestations of miracles. They are *stages* of consciousness, rather than *states* of consciousness. A stage must be earned, whereas a state can be brought on artificially through taking a chemical substance for example, or through a sustained meditative discipline. Higher stages of consciousness can come about only through self-discipline and grace. They are out of the reach of the grasping ego.

Such stages are not about gaining powers, they're about self-realisation. Look at the words for some of the Siddhis – Devotion, Wisdom, Being, Mastery; these aren't powers, they are manifestations of unity. When someone reaches one of these stages, they experience the same realisation. They discover that there is no personal 'I', no individuality anymore. There is only everything and there is nothing, and in that everything, there is also a distinct flavour or fragrance; it is the same icing, but in each of us it has a different flavour.

Thus, spiritual teachers often give contradictory advice. How do you know which teacher or which teaching to follow? If you could see the genetic makeup of your Siddhis, the flavour of your own enlightenment, you would be able to clearly answer this question. You could open yourself up to that without being confused by other paths or other teachers that don't match your inner being.

Again, here is unique wisdom. You needn't believe me; you can try this out for yourself. Use your intuition, it is much more trustworthy than I am. I can trust my own intuitive guidance system, but it's really just for me. Your intuition is your guidance system. Listen deeply to it and trust what it tells you.

CULTIVATION AND CONTEMPLATION

There are two ways to open up to these higher states and you will need both. The first way of opening to the higher states is simply to contemplate them. That may sound simple, even perhaps trite, but make no mistake, contemplation is powerful. I will share in this book what I mean by contemplation. You can look into your Gene Keys profile and see the Siddhis imprinted from birth; or you can pick one at random from the Spectrum, one that you like the feel and sound of. Follow your intuition. When it comes to the higher states and stages there can be no rules. You then contemplate that Siddhi and you identify and immerse yourself in its makeup.

Let's say you choose Ecstasy, the 46th Siddhi. You might like to begin by thinking about any time in your life when you experienced ecstasy for a few moments, even for a flash, and bring back that memory. It might be a moment of utter joy or the moment of orgasm or when you first saw your newborn child. The first thing to recognise is that you have within you the capacity to re-experience this ecstasy. Then – like a gardener – with your imagination, you cultivate and contemplate that feeling. You think about it, you dream of it, you imagine yourself and your life in that state.

How different would your life look from within that state? Bring that memory alive. You might also research renowned saints who experienced ecstasy. You make ecstasy your field of expertise. Of course, you'll notice how 99% of the time you don't feel ecstasy, but that's where you begin. You begin with honesty and you begin with an open mind.

The mind is a very powerful tool. The mind gets a bad rap in the spiritual world these days, but there's an old esoteric law – energy follows thought – that the thing that you think about the most, you eventually become. You can thus use the mind in committing yourself to this subject, this Siddhi. If you are persistent, then within a short space of time you will experience a burst of ecstasy. When this happens, the experience gets anchored in your physical DNA as a memory. Then you go on watering that memory like a seed, and over time it grows. One day this shoot reaches into your emotional life and starts to affect the way you see others.

You become more forgiving since you now know you have this flowering inside you. You no longer need to put such pressure on others to make you happy, so your relationships become lighter and more beautiful. You begin to find your own fuel instead of looking for it always *out there*, in the outside world.

This is just one example of how contemplation works. It is an ancient technique used by mystics for millennia. It takes commitment, but it works. That's the first way to taste the siddhic state.

The second way goes deeper because the second way stabilises the '*state*' into a '*stage*'. If you only use contemplation on the Siddhi, you'll get high, but you won't be able to ground that state for any long period of time. I'd go so far as to say that contemplation on the Siddhi alone can be dangerous. Many people miss this important counsel. Focussing only on the higher states can make you ungrounded and can stress your nervous system.

This is why the Gene Keys gives you a fail-safe way to access heightened states of consciousness. The way is first of all to enter the Shadow. To some of us that may sound weird. Why would we look for the higher state of consciousness in the lower vibration? Because that is where it is hidden. There is a good reason for this beautiful paradox. Our higher purpose in life is to transform these shadow patterns into their equivalent gifts and finally into their equivalent siddhis.

This may look like a long journey, but it isn't. It is simply the only journey. You start at the base and you work your way up. You can't do it from the top down. This involves using your daily life as your muse, as your means of transformation. You must learn to take responsibility for every inner state you feel, and you must learn to stop playing into other people's negative patterns. You have to transform your suffering from the inside out.

THE GOLDEN PATH

This is what the Golden Path is all about. The Golden Path is the journey through the Gene Keys of your Profile. It guides you step-by-step through this process of inner transformation. If you're interested in these higher states, if you truly wish to access them, then please look at the Golden Path programme on the Gene Keys website or obtain the book. You have to do it in stages and explore it thoroughly. It is the only way you can enter this higher realm with real safety.

So, these are the two paths in one. First, you contemplate those higher states, you begin to dream that they could be and will be you, one day. And over time you begin to realise that it isn't in the future, it's right now. You are that eternal nature.

Secondly, you begin your shadow work. The two ways go together at the same time. This teaching – *Dare to Be Divine* – is also a perfect partner to the Golden Path. For most of us, it is a huge stretch to see ourselves through a divine lens, so this gives us a real boost.

For those of us who don't find it such a stretch, who identify with these states more easily, I also offer a warning. Be sure you do your shadow work. There's a modern tendency to run ahead before we're ready. We all too easily rush towards the light while our lives are still a mess. And then we expect the light to come and clean it all up. It doesn't work that way.

You have to clean up your life first, you have to do the grounding work, you must clean out your relationships and get your health stable, and you have to sort out your finances. Then you are ready.

Happily, the Golden Path will help you with these foundation stages. You will also find a great deal of support from the Gene Keys community in following that path, so please consider visiting our website (genekeys.com) and finding out more.

DARE TO BE DIVINE

In *Dare to Be Divine*, we will therefore be exploring each of the 64 Siddhis. Through a mystical code that I will share, I'll group them in fours. Those four groups of four siddhis make sixteen, and each of these sixteen groupings of four represents a dare, a specific dare to be divine. These dares have been sent to humanity from on high... So we have sixteen dares. As an example, the first dare is:

Dare to See the Beauty in Everything.

The four Siddhis making up that dare, issue the challenge of stretching your heart open to see yourself, others, and life as beautiful. You are even dared to see that which appears ugly as beautiful, just as Mother Teresa saw the lame and wounded souls in Calcutta as 'Christ in his many distressing disguises'.

As we journey through all 64 Siddhis, you may find that you may not resonate with them all with equal ease, but it's a phenomenal opportunity to contemplate all the higher stages of consciousness possible for humanity. The journey will inevitably lead us into our collective future, and I shall share stories, possibilities, and insights about the meaning of each siddhi.

It is recommended that you study this teaching over the course of a year, with particular focus on the equinoxes and the solstices. Ideally, you will use both the webinars and the book alongside each other. Each part is coded to harmonise with the frequencies of nature as it moves through the seasons. Don't worry about which hemisphere you're in or when to begin. Just begin in whichever season you happen to be in. It works either way round but in each quarter of the year, you'll have four dares to contemplate, through sixteen different siddhis. By the time you have done them all, you'll have something profound to think about.

Perhaps you can already see how this programme is here to stretch us to our limits. It's designed to blow your mind and heart open. That is the only reason for doing it. So, prepare yourself, begin the Golden Path if you haven't already, and start to prepare the soil for these new seeds.

The final thing I'd like to share about Dare to be Divine is something magical and mystical. As we enter into a collective contemplation of these higher states, we're entering a living field of wisdom. This may have an effect on your life. In the higher states and dimensions, there are independent cosmic forces – some call them angels, some call them master bodhisattvas. They gather around wisdom such as this.

The adventure comes with grace. This process may throw things up in your life more quickly than might normally occur. This is all grist for the mill of transmutation. If you have anything hidden inside, it will be revealed. So please tread respectfully. We are walking sacred ground. The real beauty of the journey is that it isn't really about the future, it's about the now. You can't leave the now, none of us can – it's our eternal home.

Let us, therefore, be in *satsang* with the Siddhis. We will sit with them and sip them together, like fine tea.

In satsang we sit with the Master – we hang out with the Siddhis – we entertain them and we bask in their field.

In a way, this adventure tricks your attention towards the higher possibility which is already within you. It requires your yearning. It calls out your deepest dreams to know your true self.

Please prepare yourself, and if you're serious about going into this wisdom then I recommend you get your Profile and you begin the Golden Path. That will give you the basic grounding you need to understand shadow work and how transformational it can be. It may take a year to fully contemplate this teaching but this will be a deeply transformational year in your life.

The final purpose of this programme is far more collective in nature – it is to encourage us, whoever and wherever we are, to create the foundations of a global unity based on these Siddhis. This is something the world has never yet seen.

ORIENTATION

Dare To Be Divine

ORIENTATION

Before we enter into this profound set of teachings there are some things I'd like to share which are more technical in origin. They concern the basis of the transmission itself and its relationship to the Chinese I Ching. I want to keep this part separate so that the transmission stream remains uncluttered with intellectual information. The following orientation isn't very long, but it is important to get a mental grasp of the formulas involved so that you can let go into the stream and enjoy its magic. If you aren't interested in this technical part that is fine also. It is not essential to 'get' it.

As you probably know, the Gene Keys are based on the I Ching, and the I Ching mirrors our DNA's genetic code. The grid or pattern of the 64 hexagrams is a universal coding system that underpins the whole of creation.

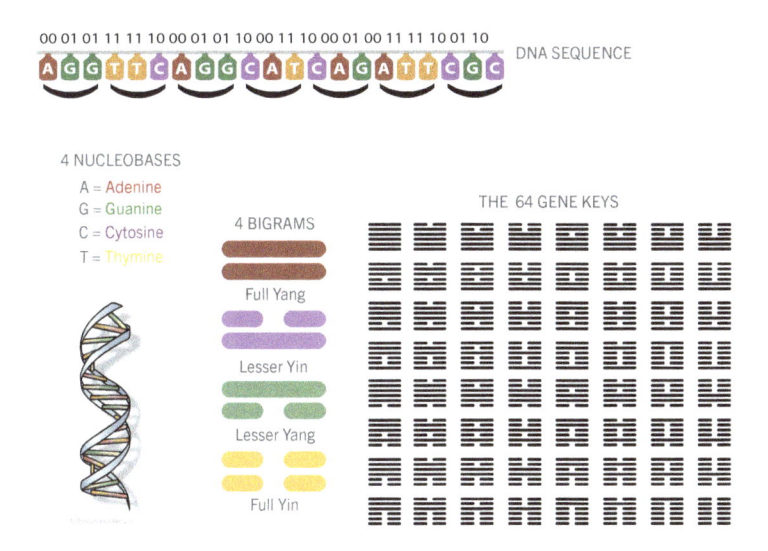

The I Ching is based on the fundamental binary nature of our perceived universe, whose building blocks are made out of opposites. In the I Ching these are represented by yin and yang.

Yang is an unbroken line and yin is represented by a line with a break in the middle. Yang is broadly male and yin, female.

When you combine these symbols in turn, you see four possible interactions of yin and yang: yin/yang, yang/yin, yin/yin, and yang/yang. These are called the four bigrams. They mirror the genetic code, where they're known as the four bases, the essential chemical components of all organic life.

In the I Ching, you can then take this a stage further by combining the yin/yang symbols into threes; these are called trigrams and create eight possible permutations.

In DNA these are called triplets – they are base combinations built out of three's, each one coding for a different amino acid. These triplets, when paired together into sixes, then create 64 possible combinations.

In the I Ching, the same sixes are created from two trigram combinations, one on top of the other. The possible combinations are numbered 1-64, and they are called hexagrams.

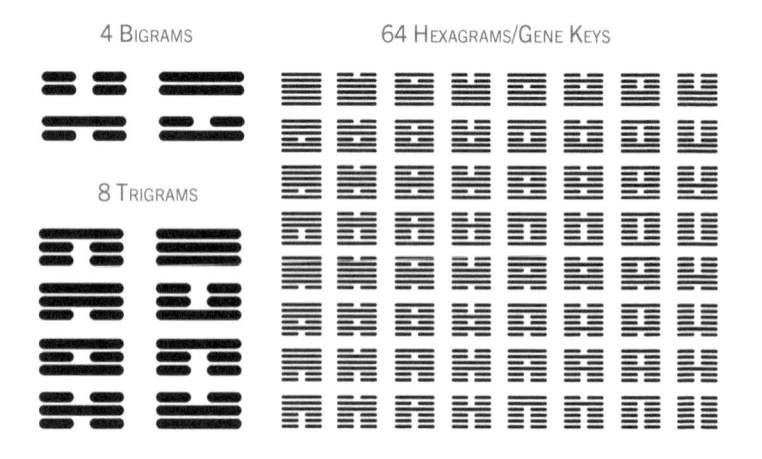

4 Bigrams

8 Trigrams

64 Hexagrams/Gene Keys

That is the basis of the I Ching and a little bit of its relationship to DNA. The same code could be explored in other areas, such as music, through the eight octaves (another 64), or through sacred geometry, by exploring the Phi ratio. There are many openings to explore through this code. In this teaching, I am using the I Ching as a means of exploring consciousness – that's what the Gene Keys really are. They're a way of mapping universal harmonics in your life.

	SHADOW	GIFT	SIDDHI		SHADOW	GIFT	SIDDHI
1	Entropy	Freshness	Beauty	33	Forgetting	Mindfulness	Revelation
2	Dislocation	Orientation	Unity	34	Force	Strength	Majesty
3	Chaos	Innovation	Innocence	35	Hunger	Adventure	Boundlessness
4	Intolerance	Understanding	Forgiveness	36	Turbulence	Humanity	Compassion
5	Impatience	Patience	Timelessness	37	Weakness	Equality	Tenderness
6	Conflict	Diplomacy	Peace	38	Struggle	Perseverance	Honour
7	Division	Guidance	Virtue	39	Provocation	Dynamism	Liberation
8	Mediocrity	Style	Exquisiteness	40	Exhaustion	Resolve	Divine Will
9	Inertia	Determination	Invincibility	41	Fantasy	Anticipation	Emanation
10	Self-Obsession	Naturalness	Being	42	Expectation	Detachment	Celebration
11	Obscurity	Idealism	Light	43	Deafness	Insight	Epiphany
12	Vanity	Discrimination	Purity	44	Interference	Teamwork	Synarchy
13	Discord	Discernment	Empathy	45	Dominance	Synergy	Communion
14	Compromise	Competence	Bounteousness	46	Seriousness	Delight	Ecstasy
15	Dullness	Magnetism	Florescence	47	Oppression	Transmutation	Transfiguration
16	Indifference	Versatility	Mastery	48	Inadequacy	Resourcefulness	Wisdom
17	Opinion	Far-Sightedness	Omniscience	49	Reaction	Revolution	Rebirth
18	Judgement	Integrity	Perfection	50	Corruption	Equilibrium	Harmony
19	Co-Dependence	Sensitivity	Sacrifice	51	Agitation	Initiative	Awakening
20	Superficiality	Self-Assurance	Presence	52	Stress	Restraint	Stillness
21	Control	Authority	Valour	53	Immaturity	Expansion	Superabundance
22	Dishonour	Graciousness	Grace	54	Greed	Aspiration	Ascension
23	Complexity	Simplicity	Quintessence	55	Victimisation	Freedom	Freedom
24	Addiction	Invention	Silence	56	Distraction	Enrichment	Intoxication
25	Constriction	Acceptance	Universal Love	57	Unease	Intuition	Clarity
26	Pride	Artfulness	Invisibility	58	Dissatisfaction	Vitality	Bliss
27	Selfishness	Altruism	Selflessness	59	Dishonesty	Intimacy	Transparency
28	Purposelessness	Totality	Immortality	60	Limitation	Realism	Justice
29	Half-Heartedness	Commitment	Devotion	61	Psychosis	Inspiration	Sanctity
30	Desire	Lightness	Rapture	62	Intellect	Precision	Impeccability
31	Arrogance	Leadership	Humility	63	Doubt	Inquiry	Truth
32	Failure	Preservation	Veneration	64	Confusion	Imagination	Illumination

THE NUCLEAR HEXAGRAMS

As you may know, through the Gene Keys *Spectrum of Consciousness* we have a map of how these higher harmonics work. At their highest level, they are called the 64 Siddhis, which are the basis of *Dare to be Divine*. These 64 words for the Siddhis describe a human life in perfect harmony with the cosmos.

There are many more codes hidden in the I Ching. One of my personal favourites is called the nuclear hexagrams, which is the base of this particular teaching. The nuclear hexagrams are a code within a code. Hidden within each of the 64 hexagrams is another secret hexagram – this is known as a *nuclear hexagram*. Here's how it works:

How To Form a Nuclear Hexagram

Example: Hexagram 63

Here you can see the 63rd hexagram made up of two hidden trigrams called the *nuclear trigrams*. Counting the six lines from the bottom, you can see that the first trigram is the one made up of lines 3, 4, and 5. That's called the *upper nuclear trigram*. The second one is made up of lines 2, 3, and 4. That's the *lower nuclear trigram*.

If you then take these two new trigrams and place them together, they form a whole new hexagram. This being the hidden essence of the 63rd hexagram, is called its nuclear hexagram. In this case, it happens to be the 64th hexagram which is the programming partner of the 63rd hexagram, but it isn't the same way for all of them. When you calculate the nuclear patterns through the whole I Ching, some very interesting themes and correspondences occur.

We will look at another one, just to make the principle clear.

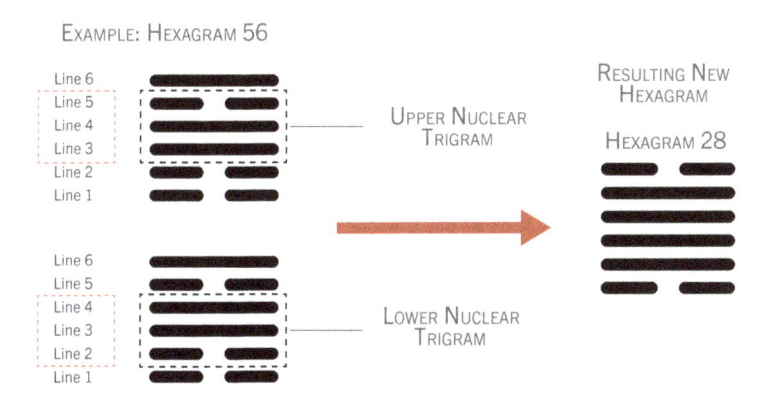

EXAMPLE: HEXAGRAM 56

Line 6
Line 5
Line 4
Line 3
Line 2
Line 1

UPPER NUCLEAR TRIGRAM

RESULTING NEW HEXAGRAM

HEXAGRAM 28

Line 6
Line 5
Line 4
Line 3
Line 2
Line 1

LOWER NUCLEAR TRIGRAM

Here you can see the 56th hexagram with its upper nuclear trigram, yang/yang/yin, and the lower nuclear hexagram, yin/yang/yang. When you bring these two together you get a new hexagram, which in this case, is hexagram 28. In other words, within Gene Key 56 is hidden Gene Key 28.

Hopefully, you now understand the basic formula. The next part of this orientation is about what happens when you use this formula on all 64 of the Gene Keys.

An amazing pattern emerges. When you uncover the nuclear hexagrams of each of the 64, you discover that you can reduce the essence of the 64 into sixteen. Each of these sixteen nuclear hexagrams represents four other hexagrams and the total of 16x4 is 64, so what you're looking at is the essence hidden within the I Ching – a code within a code.

Furthermore, if you repeat the process with these sixteen hexagrams, looking inside each one for its nuclear hexagram, guess what happens? You get down to four.

These are the four base hexagrams of the entire I Ching. Thus I call them the *4 Pillars*. Inside every hexagram is a code and hidden inside that code is another code. In this way the I Ching is a fractal pattern.

THE 4 ESSENTIAL HEXAGRAMS/GENE KEYS

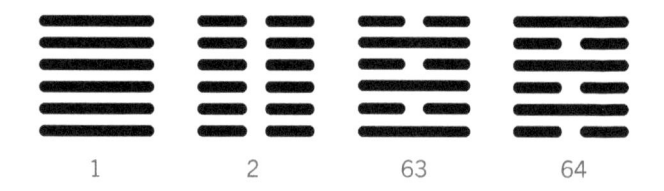

| 1 | 2 | 63 | 64 |

This is a hidden language, which you will see throughout this teaching. In the column on the facing page, you'll see what I call the *48 Letters*. These are the outermost hexagrams of the I Ching.

In the middle column, you can see the nuclear hexagrams that emerge from each of these 48. For example, hexagrams 30, 55, 56, and 62 are a family, because they all contain the nuclear hexagram number 28. However, when you look at the middle column you see that the 28 and the 43, and the 44 are also a family, each containing the six yang lines of nuclear hexagram number 1.

In this way the whole I Ching can be condensed down to these four primary hexagrams – the 1, 2, 63, and 64 – the bookends of the I Ching. They represent the Alpha and the Omega –

the beginning and the end. The centre column is called the *12 Mysteries* because it contains all manner of open secrets.

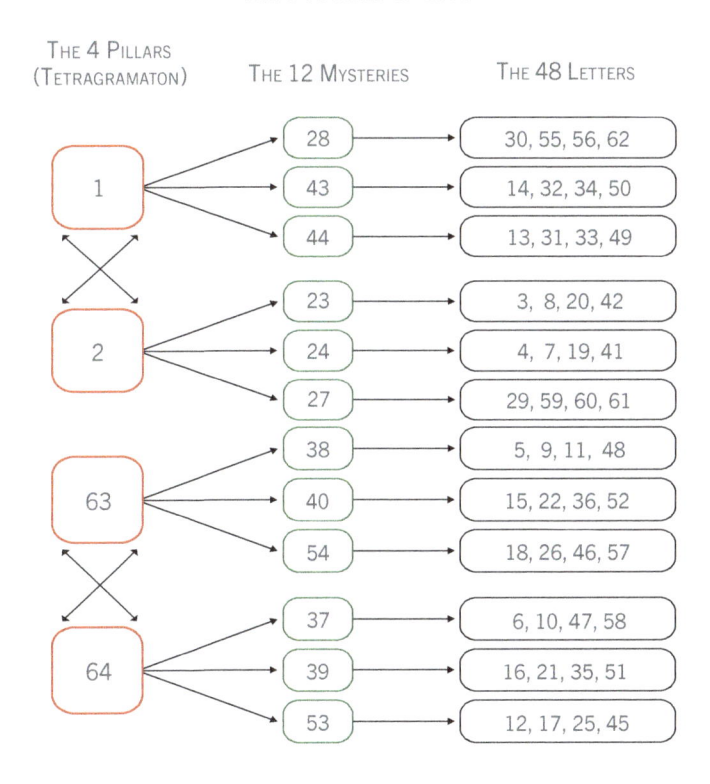

THE 64 NAMES OF LOVE

THE 4 PILLARS (TETRAGRAMATON)	THE 12 MYSTERIES	THE 48 LETTERS
1	28	30, 55, 56, 62
	43	14, 32, 34, 50
	44	13, 31, 33, 49
2	23	3, 8, 20, 42
	24	4, 7, 19, 41
	27	29, 59, 60, 61
63	38	5, 9, 11, 48
	40	15, 22, 36, 52
	54	18, 26, 46, 57
64	37	6, 10, 47, 58
	39	16, 21, 35, 51
	53	12, 17, 25, 45

The column on the right is called the *48 Letters* because these 48 hexagrams form the main *Divine Alphabet* out of which all the Names of Love are formed.

The I Ching is filled with hidden codes, just as life is. Don't worry if you didn't understand anything so far, for it will come clear. The main purpose of this teaching is to bring this code alive in your life. As you will see, it is the code to our higher evolution.

Part 1

The First Four Dares

The Sacred Letters of Light

DARE TO BE DIVINE

THE SACRED LETTERS OF LIGHT

We saw in the orientation that the entire I Ching can be reduced down to these four Gene Keys. The 1, the 2, the 63, and the 64, together contain the entire code of life in microcosm. Every other hexagram, every other Gene Key, all sixty of them, lie hidden within these four.

These four sacred Pillars – the Letters of Light – are what the Cabalists called the Tetragrammaton – the four-fold name of God – *Yod Heh Vav Heh.*

For us, studying the Gene Keys, they are the Siddhis of Beauty, Unity, Truth, and Illumination.

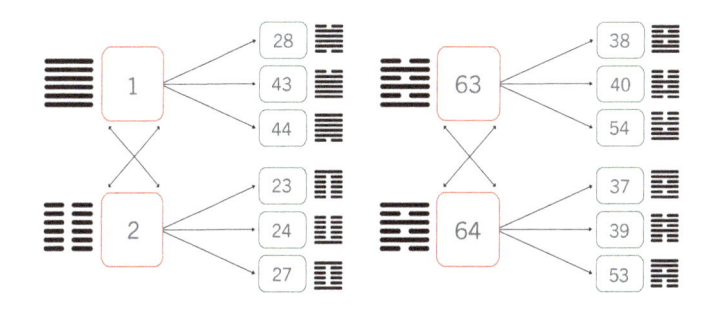

Within each of these four Gene Keys are hidden three others, making sixteen in total.

In 1 are hidden 28, 43, 44.

In 2 are hidden 23, 24, 27.

In 63 are hidden 38, 40, 54.

In 64 are hidden 37, 39, 53.

So these 12 Mysteries Gene Keys are also special. We are going to explore them in their natural groups of four, and each of these four contains a dare.

THE FIRST DARE – DARE TO SEE THE BEAUTY IN EVERYTHING

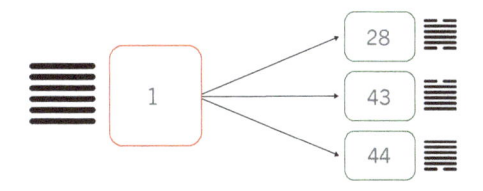

THE 1 – **BEAUTY** – BEAUTY IS ALWAYS NEW

THE 28 – **IMMORTALITY** – BEAUTY IS FOREVER

THE 43 – **EPIPHANY** – TRUE BEAUTY LIES WITHIN

THE 44 – **SYNARCHY** – BEAUTY CANNOT EXIST IN ISOLATION

THE 1ST SIDDHI – BEAUTY

Beauty is Always New

This is the Siddhi of Beauty. It's the first hexagram, the first Gene Key in the entire I Ching. All six lines are yang, so it's all fire, all creativity. This is the creative evolutionary impulse itself.

Beauty is a strange quality, as it's not really of this world. Beauty is ephemeral – its nature cannot be captured or fixed here on Earth.

Beauty comes in fleeting moments – it's here one minute and it's gone in the next. As one of the four pillars, beauty is a fundamental principle of divinity.

What we can say is that Beauty is related to the element of Fire. I love the way the Sun is in this 1st Gene Key around the fifth of November, and here in the UK at least, we gather round and light big bonfires to celebrate Guy Fawkes Night – a revolutionary who tried to bring down the government by blowing up the Houses of Parliament! Regardless of this ludicrous custom, this is still traditionally a time, as autumn entering winter turns the leaves to gold, for many fire festivals.

Think about these Siddhis and how rare they are. There have been so few truly awakened beings in our world. We have only a smattering to serve as examples. It is hard to find such a one representing the Siddhi of Beauty. One whom I can imagine is Zarathustra.

NICHOLAS ROERICH, *ZARATHUSTRA* (1931)

Zarathustra, from ancient Persia, is an almost mythical prophet. Little is known of him. He was a great lover of the sacred fire and it is said that he brought fire down from the heavens. He must have been an extraordinary man, a Promethean avatar.

And perhaps since the time of Zarathustra, many thousands of years ago, we have seen no other example of this fundamental Siddhi. That is something to contemplate. When this Siddhi comes into the world, then the world must change. It must become more beautiful, more energised, and more transformed.

At around the same time as Zarathustra, many other beautiful beings also incarnated – Buddha, Mahavir, Lao Tzu – these great beings from other, higher dimensions. My hunch is that Zarathustra opened the door for beauty to pour through from the inner planes onto the Earth. Even today, the fire is still coming.

These Siddhis manifest in degrees. A person carrying this in his/her DNA (in other words in their profile) is guided by its fiery power. These are people with vast creative reserves. They are here to beautify the world. That's what the 1st Gift of Freshness does. But the Siddhi turns that creative power inwards – to pierce through into the realm of the gods, into the dimensionless realm where beauty can be embodied, rather than being known only fleetingly through the senses.

This then is our first dare – Dare to see everything as beautiful. To see everything as beautiful you will have to go through the Fire of Transformation. That is what suffering does on this human plane – it purifies us. It washes us clean.

This has been misinterpreted by so many. There is no need to go looking for suffering. It comes inevitably with these vehicles. But to use its energy to create something of beauty – a life of beauty – that is surely the revolutionary purpose of life. We are here to learn to see beauty even in ugliness. We are here to see the perfection of the universe playing out in every conceivable way.

We will need to talk quite a bit during this teaching about the nature of incarnation. How can we not? We incarnate into this turning wheel of 'samsara'. We live within a hologram, and we come into the hologram on different axes, at different angles. The ancients called our celestial centre the *axis mundi*. From it, we play out our incarnative games here on Earth. It all depends on the angle we come in at, and that angle is all based on timing.

Your Hologenetic Profile reveals this special knowledge of the pattern of your incarnation. So to see beauty, you need to embody the deepest aspects of your profile.

Beauty is a revelation underlying creation. However, it doesn't yet exist here on Earth as form. We are insufficiently equipped to know beauty in our present bodies. When the Great Change has finished with us – this great sea-change that's coming to our planet – then we shall be better aligned with what beauty truly is.

This 1st Siddhi hides within it three other Siddhis – the 28, the 43, and the 44. If we want to perceive the Siddhi of Beauty, we should look at these three and their insights.

The first insight then is that beauty is always new. This means that within the illusion of time, on the material plane, outer beauty must always be ephemeral.

THE 28TH SIDDHI – IMMORTALITY
Beauty is Forever

The second insight comes from the 28th Siddhi – Immortality.

Outside time, beauty is eternal. It's forever. How can beauty be both ephemeral and eternal? Why – this is a Siddhi, a paradoxical divine state.

Immortality is a word that most humans don't have much time for in our everyday lives. However, immortality is our nature. We cannot die. Our consciousness is eternal. The body dies, but not the in-dwelling awareness, and just like beauty, immortality has no objective existence on our planet at this time.

There are people who managed to extend the life of the body, but probably not for very long. There is talk, in fact quite well documented, of a 250-year-old man in China. But physical immortality? We haven't seen it yet.

Whenever a person discovers enlightenment they realise their immortality. That is why they seem so at peace. To dare to see the world as beautiful is to contemplate your eternity.

We come into and out of this wheel. We are born, we die, and then we are born again. All of this takes place without our remembering that we are immortal. We are God at play, forgetting ourselves so that we can have this game of evolution. And yet from outside the game, the game is seen for what it is – a divine *lila* – a sport for the gods. There is great beauty to it, and when we remember and embrace eternity, suddenly the whole pattern seems more playful and more beautiful.

This 28th Gene Key governs a series of codes within the body which, once initiated, lead to a by-passing of the ordinary ageing process. Not only can we extend our age, but we have the capacity to do so indefinitely. The ability of the body to rebuild itself is already known. Thus, it's not such a leap to realise that physical immortality is one day going to be our norm. Many of us cannot imagine such a thing – to live forever in this physical body? But it won't be in this body. It will be in a body that has transcended time and space. For most people that is unimaginable – we have to open our minds to these Siddhis.

THE 43RD SIDDHI – EPIPHANY
True Beauty Lies Within

This brings us to the 43rd Siddhi – Epiphany.

As a species, our greatest journeys remain untrodden. We still have hardly ventured within. We are just getting started. Epiphany is what happens when we discover our eternal nature through going within.

Epiphany is a Siddhi that triggers sudden memory. This is the tradition of sudden enlightenment – Paul on the road to Damascus, Eckhart Tolle's sudden awakening in his bedroom.

The 43rd Siddhi may be significant somewhere in the Profiles of all those who have sudden breakthroughs.

Epiphany dawns when Immortality breaks through and the personal self is shown to be false. If you have the 43 in your Profile or are mysteriously drawn to it, then you can never be prepared for awakening. The 43rd Gene Key is the secret passage that suddenly implodes into the higher realms.

Such breakthroughs of the Siddhis may not occur for everyone. This is not up to you either. It's all part of the pattern of destiny that lies out of our hands. At the gift frequency, we may seem to hold the reins. We are busy about our lives, at being a success, a failure, or whatever agenda we are following, but at the Siddhi level, nothing lies in our hands.

There are small breakthroughs and there are great ones. We can do things to seduce or invite the small breakthroughs like contemplation, meditation, and prayer but the great ones? They only ever happen once. Thus we must go within, and that is the role of the 43rd Gene Key. We simply cannot imagine the vastness of the beauty that we will find until we look inside our hearts.

THE 44TH SIDDHI – SYNARCHY
Beauty Cannot Exist in Isolation

Finally, we come to the 44th Gene Key – Synarchy. Beauty cannot exist in isolation. Beauty is found in the way that things connect to each other.

Beauty is found in Synarchy – where we come together. In the I Ching, the 44th hexagram is called *Coming to Meet*. We keep coming down here to Earth to meet one another. Beauty thus has a hidden purpose to bring us together. We will go on incarnating until we can see our beauty, our inherent unity. As long as a single person exists who believes we are separate, we will all keep coming here.

Synarchy is another unusual Siddhi. It aligns us to a wider hierarchical waveband – to levels of collective consciousness that are far beyond us – the Ascended Masters, the Illuminati, the Great White Brotherhood, and Sisterhood – to the angelic realms.

This is a collective Siddhi. It exerts a pressure in all human beings – to try and model ourselves on this higher structural harmony. The 44th Gift is Teamwork because that is where Synarchy begins. But the Siddhi is our real future.

One day we will come into Synarchy.

One day we will all have the Epiphany.

One day we will all realise our Immortality.

First, we have to learn to see the beauty even in corruption and interference, which is the shadow of this Gene Key.

I realise I may be taken to task for such words. Everyone under the sun is a part of the pattern, no matter how corrupt they appear. Sometimes the pattern as a whole needs to reveal its shadow side in more depth in order for everyone to see and address it more clearly.

Synarchy is where we are headed. Look at the sun if you want to know what synarchy is. The sun is humanity in the far future. All of those beings that make up the sun have known epiphany and now express the divine fire of their beauty in perfect synarchy. It is so beautiful that you cannot even see them anymore. All you see is one great being of fire and light and warmth. We are blinded by the sheer beauty of that incomprehensible light.

So, consider your life, and try to see the beauty that's all around you. See where life is, and wonder at its aching beauty. Know that a million years from now, perfection like the sun will have been achieved. And then just enjoy the whole process for what it is and for where it is.

THE SECOND DARE – DARE TO BE THE ONE

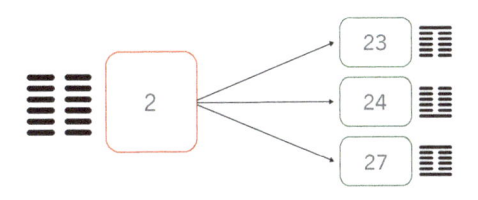

THE 2 – **UNITY** – OUR UNFALLEN STATE

THE 23 – **QUINTESSENCE** – LOVE IS THE 5TH ELEMENT

THE 24 – **SILENCE** – ONENESS IS A SILENT MIND

THE 27 – **SELFLESSNESS** – THE DOCTRINE OF HARMLESSNESS

THE 2ND SIDDHI – UNITY

Our Unfallen State

The 1st and 2nd Siddhis are a pair – they are programming partners. With Beauty, we had the primary yang, which is Fire, the 'creative'. Now we have the primary yin, Water, the 'receptive', the feminine.

The 2nd Gene Key holds a profound story. Its Shadow is Dislocation. It is about being lost. We are lost souls – that's how we begin here on Earth. We are here to remember our Unity, and the Gift here is Orientation. We can find and correct our course by learning to accept the flow of our lives. Behind it, all is the state of unity. Isn't that something to consider? In general, people out in the world don't have this insight, which can cause deep relaxation in your inner being. Unity is our unfallen state. It's our home. This Siddhi is all about homecoming. That's why it's the Great Mother Gene Key, the great feminine.

What do we mean by Dare to be the One? We mean 'the chosen one'. If you want to connect back to your original unity, you must change the way you appear in the script of your life.

Why be a follower when you can be a Buddha? You can be the Christ and realise yourself as the Master. That doesn't mean behaving all 'holy', which would make no difference. It means you enlarge your view of what you really are. If you can't begin to see yourself as that vast endless being, how will you let go into it at the point of death?

That's what is offered to us while we are dying. In this dare, we are practising for our death; we are preparing to become the ocean – to let it take us. Surrender yourself into the ocean of being and know that you are Unity even in your imperfection.

Like the 1st Siddhi, the 2nd Siddhi comes into the world only at great turning points. These people are the great avatars. So if you have a 2nd Siddhi or feel deeply drawn to it, then contemplate this pressure inside you to embrace the whole. You are an agent of unity. The more you give yourself to that, the more it will expand you.

I want to clarify that these Dares are for us all. It doesn't matter what is in your Profile. Your Profile can be a focal point for your contemplation, but when we expand our awareness like this, we sometimes have to leave the maps behind. Dare to be the one. Dare to encompass vastness.

Now let's take a look at the nuclear Siddhis inside the 2nd Siddhi...

THE 23RD SIDDHI – QUINTESSENCE
Love is the Fifth Element

Love is the 5th element. This is what Quintessence means. The fifth element is ether. It's a distillation of the other four elements – earth, air, fire, and water.

The fifth element represents our refined essence. Life teaches us this alchemy – to use the dirty cloth of our suffering to polish the lens of our awareness until it shines. Then the Quintessence glows – within our eyes and our belly, as unconditional love. This is the love that binds all things and all beings together as One.

To know your quintessence is to know your role in the cosmic drama – whether it's a global role or a simpler, local role – for all roles make up the whole.

The Quintessence is the same in each of us. It is not about what we do. It is the presence we bring into the world.

The 23rd Siddhi unlocks the power of the thyroid gland, which has mystical capacities. The one who distills the essence of their life force activates these higher capacities. Then the human voice can be used as a means of manipulating matter.

At lower levels of frequency, the 23rd Gene Key can manipulate people's feelings. Many 23's are orators, comedians, radio DJs, and politicians. But at the highest level, one can vibrate the Quintessence. If you can vibrate this Quintessence inside you, then you can vibrate it within anything because it lies at the heart of all things.

This Siddhi can bend matter to its will. Only he or she who has entered the heart of the Divine can bend matter to God's will. This is the origin of this hexagram's name – *Splitting Apart*. One can split open the atomic structure and bend it to one's will – all through the power of the voice.

THE 24TH SIDDHI – SILENCE
Oneness is a Silent Mind

This is the exact opposite of the 23. In the 23, the power is in the speaking, whereas in the 24 the power is in not speaking. This is the Siddhi of Silence – Oneness is a silent mind.

The voice ascends; the silence *descends*. Only in silence do we hear the Word. Only in silence are we truly together. Many mystics have demonstrated the power of this Siddhi. By not speaking, one cannot be distracted by words. The quintessence then begins to communicate and the aura does the talking. When you share time with a silent mind, your mind falls silent. True silence is contagious.

RAMANA MAHARSHI

I imagine that when Ramana Maharshi went into silence at his ashram in Southern India, the silence was so vast and all-encompassing that entire villages and towns were affected. And if you go there even today, the silence remains, imprinted in the rocks of the holy mountain Arunachala.

THE 27TH SIDDHI — SELFLESSNESS
The Doctrine of Harmlessness

Unity is founded upon altruism. The glue of unity is goodness. The 23 takes you to the centre, you then fall silent in the 24, and finally, you learn to serve through the 27. Service must flow from silence, from our centre. If it does not, it does more harm than good.

The great teachers of meditation are often asked the same question: what about the world? There is so much suffering. What can we do? Just meditating doesn't seem enough. It isn't helping the world!

The answers are resoundingly similar: how can you help when you do not know? How can you be selfless when you are filled with concerns of the self? If you don't transcend the self, you will only approach the symptoms and never reach the root of the world's problems.

This is why so many teachers have begun with this simple instruction: *do no harm*. Do no harm begins to clear out your aura. Do no harm means that you begin to consider the feelings of others and the creatures we share the world with. You consider what you say, how you think, and how you act. Can you move through a single day without doing any harm to anyone or anything?

This is how we learn to see the self in action. We must see first our selfishness. Many try to serve out of selfishness – to escape their suffering, or for recognition. True service is not a career choice, it is an overflowing of compassionate love.

This 27th Siddhi is one of the great Siddhis of healing. Here we find the possibility of miraculous healing through the field of unity.

There is a story by Swami Rama, of his Master in the Himalayas. He went one day to visit a very sick devotee of his Master.

The man had a terrible affliction, with large purple blotches and boils all over his body. He was very near death. Swami recounts how he stood fascinated while his Master walked around the sick man three times and chanted some words. He then watched in real-time as the boils began to disappear and the man recovered. Then the Master went outside, and Swami noticed that the boils were appearing on his Master.

However, his Master then transferred the illness into a large tree. Swami even saw the boils appear briefly on the tree trunk before disappearing. This experience was one of the turning points of his young life.

The 27th Siddhi has this kind of capacity to heal, to take on the karma of others, and transmute it. This is the ultimate gesture of selfless love.

Dare to be the One. Dare to live a great life. Expand your capacity to love.

Cultivate your essence. Then offer it to others as service.

The Second Dare

THE THIRD DARE — DARE TO BE TRUTHFUL

Now we come to the second pairing of hexagrams – the bookends at the end of the I Ching, the 63rd, and the 64th Gene Keys.

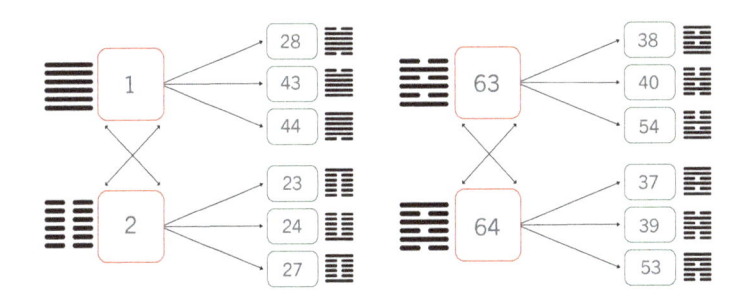

We have had Beauty and Unity, and now we have Truth and Illumination. These Four Letters of Light sound out the name of God.

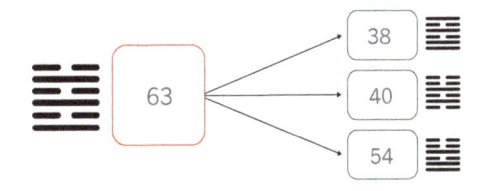

THE 63 – **TRUTH** – ABSOLUTE TRUTH IS COLLECTIVE

THE 38 – **HONOUR** – THE ETERNAL WARRIOR

THE 40 – **DIVINE WILL** – OMNIPOTENCE IN ACTION

THE 54 – **ASCENSION** – SEEK AND YE SHALL FIND

Here then is our third Dare, and a very practical one: never tell an untruth. Never tell an untruth to yourself either. Perhaps that is not so easy.

THE 63RD SIDDHI – TRUTH
Absolute Truth is Collective

The 63rd Siddhi is the great Siddhi of Truth. Absolute truth is collective: that is the key insight here. There is relative truth and there is absolute truth. Relative truth comes through an individual's inner truth. This is the truth conveyed by one who is fully realised. Absolute Truth, however, is collective. Here we find the origin of the Bodhisattva vow – 'I will hold back my full awakening and keep returning to Earth until the last human is freed'. Only when all beings are free can absolute Truth be known. As long as someone suffers somewhere, an eye is closed to Truth.

Hexagram 63 is called *After Completion*. This is a mystical name, for absolute Truth can only be known at the end, when all are awake. So this is the dare for all beings – to be honest always – absolutely. Never tell a lie. When a man or a woman tells a lie, it kills a part of the world.

This whole incarnation mystery can only be resolved when all are free; when the last curtain falls, when heaven comes to Earth. This will be one day our destiny, as certain as the fact we are here. Because the play is in full swing, the play must someday come to its conclusion.

This is the perfect hexagram pattern – yang, yin, yang, yin, yang, yin. The alternating lines are in the perfect places for harmony – hence Truth.

Mystically this is a Siddhi used by higher beings to incarnate on earth. By the way, it doesn't mean if you have your Sun there in your Profile, that you are a planetary avatar! But it may indicate that you are in some manner aligned with such beings. We each have to work our way up, through self-enquiry, through the Gift of this Gene Key, and then one day the Gift will fall open naturally into the Siddhi – into Truth.

THE 38TH SIDDHI – HONOUR
The Eternal Warrior

Once you have Truth you become a warrior. You become a force for good. The eternal warrior loves a good battle and relishes a strong adversary. Truth seeks out untruth, if that can be said; although at a certain level of frequency there is no such thing as untruth.

Truth however will always be tested. Each human life begins as a struggle, then it becomes a battle, and finally, it becomes a dance.

The Master is the ultimate warrior, the ultimate dancer. He or she is invisible. He or she has surrendered the self, so no defence is necessary anymore. Yet still the battle between light and dark, between awake and asleep goes on.

The Siddhi of Honour is to be found wherever there is still injustice, and wherever a warrior is beset by insurmountable odds. Honour is more than courage. It also encompasses justice. Honour can turn even defeat into victory. These are lives, such as Gandhi, William Wallace, or anyone who has stood for what is right against that which appears overpowering but is known to be wrong.

Dare to speak the Truth, even if it means you will be condemned. Dare to stand fast in your truth, with an open heart, and with faith in the inevitable victory of goodness over evil. Dare to take a stand. That's the 38th Siddhi. It cannot back down, and even if it dies, it will eventually always achieve its goal.

Dare to be true. Grace will follow you and it will always find you in the end; such is the nature of honour.

THE 40TH SIDDHI — DIVINE WILL
Omnipotence in Action

So we have Truth, Honour and now Will.

Perhaps you can feel this one's energy. The 40th Siddhi is all-powerful…

In the Seven Sacred Seals, a mystical branch of the Gene Keys wisdom, the 40th Siddhi is allied to the figure of Archangel Michael, who battles the dragon – the deepest aspect of our collective forgetting. Remember our insight from the 63rd Siddhi – *Absolute Truth is collective*. We all are here to fight the demons of our forgetting and our ignorance.

Divine Will resides within every Siddhi. Once we have surrendered the small self, we become the universal self. We become one with God. Not my will, but thy will be done. So, we have to surrender our individual will, our will to power. Only when we dive into the Divine can this great Siddhi work through us.

The 40th Siddhi is here to transform all fear. It works through the Grace of acceptance and surrender. It wins only because it surrenders.

These Siddhis are the multitudinous names of love. Love is nothing but the will of God. To become one with the Divine is to become an instrument of the Divine – a hollow reed.

The 40th Siddhi's touch of Grace can intervene in any human destiny and change any outcome. It is omnipotence in action. Sometimes it is also the grace of allowing things to simply follow their natural course. In time, all is revealed.

THE 54TH SIDDHI – ASCENSION
Seek and Ye Shall Find

This dare culminates in the 54th Siddhi – Ascension. Seek and ye shall find. Knock, and it shall be answered. Here is the opposite of the 40th Siddhi. The 40th asks us to surrender, but the 54th requires great effort and great resilience.

The elements making up this hexagram are lightning above and water below.

REMBRANDT, *THE STORM ON THE SEA OF GALILEE* (1633)

Instantly I am reminded of that wonderful painting by Rembrandt, of Jesus and his disciples in the storm on the sea of Galilee. A more atmospheric painting is hard to imagine. Jesus alone was undisturbed by the storm raging around him. And of course, he then spoke to the wind and the storm subsided.

There is surrender on one side, and there is personal effort on the other. To attain the higher states, we must move through effort. That is the teaching of this Gene Key. The Siddhi is our reward. It becomes an effortless effort; the paradox of surrendered effort. Truth must be won. It must be earned. And many times we will fall, but we must get up again and keep moving.

On the path of Ascension, dare to ascend. Dare to keep going against insurmountable odds. And one day, you will see. The wind will drop, the waters will calm and you will see that Grace has been following you all along.

This Siddhi calls to us – reach for the truth, it whispers – stretch for it.

This is often the renunciate's path. Yogananda has this as his Life's Work. This is the path of a Yogi. If you are graced with it, follow it and it will lead you all the way. Ascension is our eventual flowering. We will physically ascend. Several Siddhis have variations of this theme.

The false boundary that separates life and death will be transcended. It has occurred many times already. We just don't hear about it so much. Yes, we have heard the story of Jesus, but there are many more. In India, Tibet, and China, these stories are better known.

YOGANANDA

This Siddhi is the one associated with levitation. Levitation is a tale commonly told in many cultures. It is a phase of this Siddhi; when the physical body breaks the bonds of gravity.

Many people saw St Teresa of Avila levitate. There are many documented cases of saints floating above the ground. But eventually, the spirit must even transmute the physical elements. That is a different view of Ascension.

Truth leads to many new horizons. One of them is upward! So, dare to levitate.

Dare to raise your consciousness away from the bounds of the Earth. And let the Truth be your anchor.

THE FOURTH DARE – DARE TO BE ILLUMINATED

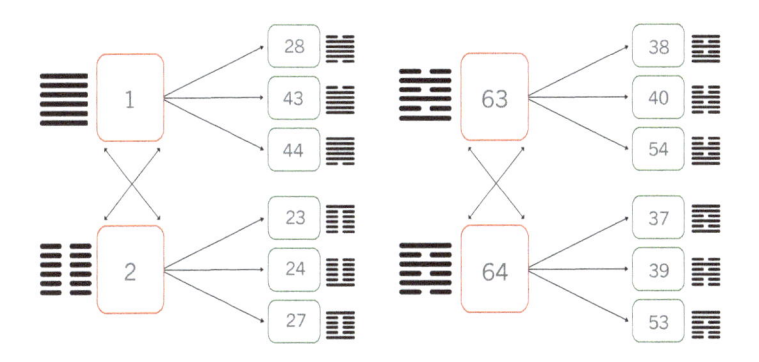

Now we come to the fourth Dare – and the final of the four Pillars upon which this sacred transmission stands – Truth and Illumination.

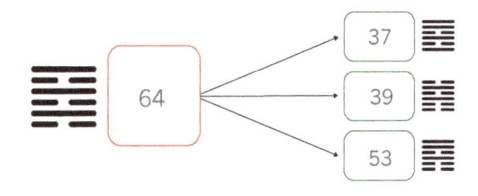

THE **64** – **ILLUMINATION** – LIGHT IS LIMITLESS

THE **39** – **LIBERATION** – UNLOCKING THE LIGHT IN YOUR DNA

THE **37** – **TENDERNESS** – THE LIGHT OF THE WORLD

THE **53** – **SUPERABUNDANCE** – HOW TO BECOME A MILLIONAIRE

THE 64TH SIDDHI – ILLUMINATION

Light is Limitless

When we think of light, we often think of it in terms of being the opposite of darkness. We believe that darkness is the absence of light. But that is not a Truth.

There can be no absence of light since light itself is limitless. This means that darkness is an illusion. We are not talking about physical light here, but the light of consciousness, the light of God. Even in our darkest moments, light is all around us. Everything is illumined. Everything is lit up from within.

There is nowhere where God is not. I would even go so far as to say that what we perceive as darkness is actually an intensification of light. It is so bright it becomes dark.

This teaching is about going beyond duality. The Siddhis are our unfallen natural state. Dare to be Illuminated means to dare to become that light, to adjust your eyes to its brightness, and to see yourself absolutely as nothing but light. Then we see only that light wherever we look.

In my Gene Keys book, I talk about the 64th Siddhi as an easel for God's imagination. We are nothing but God's thoughts. The *Spectrum of Consciousness* is just that – a palette of colours, but the Siddhis synthesise all these colours into the original white light. In higher dimensions, colours exist that are so exquisite that we would dissolve if we saw them. We perceive colour through the physical eye, but to the Siddhis there is only one eye – and therefore all colour is infinite. That is something worthy of contemplation.

There are infinite colours. These colours are God's *lilas* – God's play. They are the fractal shards of creation endlessly being created and then dissolving again. Our lives are those colours. We are a mandala. All our incarnations are creating this work of art, like a Tibetan *thangka* – our sufferings, our ecstasies, our successes, and our failures – they all go into the artwork.

Dare to be the hand that paints,

dare to be the canvas,

dare to be the paint itself. We are all of it.

Dare to be Illuminated.

THE 39TH SIDDHI – LIBERATION
Unlocking the Light in your DNA

Illumination liberates us. The 64th Gift is Imagination, which is important to understand here. The power of imagination is not the same as fantasy. In deity yoga, you picture yourself as the Buddha, the Christ, or a great Master. You entrust your creativity to unlock your inner world, your chi, your prana.

Entire systems of yoga are devoted to unlocking the inner light in our DNA. The Gene Keys are such a transmission. We use the heart-mind to open up these pathways, and at higher levels of consciousness, the mind becomes self-illuminated. It even remains awake as the body sleeps.

Dare to liberate yourself through your imagination. Allow your vast dreams to come alive inside you once again. Unblock the pathways that closed down during difficult times in your childhood. Let your heart breathe fresh, free air again. Feel the daring inside you as the rush of this new energy courses again through your veins.

You are Divine – the life divine. The Divine lives inside you, in every breath, in every movement. Free up your imagination. Cast aside the cynic, the sceptic inside you. Open to that childlike wonder as you let your mind soar, as you reach out for the Truth, as you pluck it from the heavens, as you call it into you.

You may have heard tell of great mystics or Masters who bring about sudden openings in their students in various ways. This 39th Siddhi is such a gift. We hear of a Master touching a student on their third eye or telling them to drink a glass of water and the student explodes! Such illumination occurs through this Siddhi of Liberation.

THE 37TH SIDDHI – TENDERNESS
The Light of the World

There are Siddhis that have a decidedly masculine flavour, and then there are those with a feminine touch. Here is the touch of the mother or father, and we feel it always as a parent. That is how we feel God, the Divine. We are the child. We are the lamb. We are the baby suckling at the great breast; we are held in the lap of the Divine – our Father, our Mother.

Illumination always leaves us in our hearts – in this tenderness.

Mother Julian, a great medieval mystic, calls Christ 'my Mother'. She is the first to have referred to him in that way. Many female saints carried this transmission of the 37th Siddhi, including all the avatars known as Mother or Ma – Mother Meera, Sri Anandamayi Ma, and Mother Julian herself.

And sometimes it is also the father. Meher Baba had the Sun in this Siddhi when he was born. You can see the tenderness in his eyes...

Tenderness requires supplication. It requires that we bow to the hands of the Divine above and put our trust and faith in that touch. Faith is a great part of this Siddhi. We are illuminated by Grace from above – by the gentle touch of tenderness.

MEHER BABA

The Mother is also the keeper of the maya – the prefix Ma is what holds our entire illusory world together. The mother waits for the child to grow and mature. She lets the child make mistakes – that's our karma. She lets the child learn from their karma until one day we return home to be whole again.

That is our entire journey into this world of form until we are once again fully illuminated.

Can you dare to bring that level of tenderness into your touch? Can you treat those you meet and the events of your life with that tenderness? Can you treat yourself with such tenderness?

This is a heart-opening Siddhi. Dare to come home to your own tenderness.

THE 53RD SIDDHI – SUPERABUNDANCE
How to Become a Millionaire

How to become a millionaire? I don't want to lower the tone, but after all, God has a great sense of humour. Illumination brings great expansion with it. Every time it alights on us we begin a new cycle. Superabundance is our maturity.

The joke here with millionaires is that they say if you don't have a certain figure – it used to be around 10 million and is probably a lot more now – your money isn't self-sustaining. In other words, it decreases. But at a certain figure, let's say 50 million, your money goes on expanding. It doesn't just sustain itself; it continues to grow and grow.

Light is like that. The same law is true of our inner life. Once we have released enough inner light, it begins to feed and fuel itself. Until that point, effort, exertion, and discipline are needed. Spiritual *sadhana* or practice is needed – but once the light in the aura expands to a certain level, it just takes off.

This is the state known as absorption, which follows contemplation. Absorption involves the release of inner radiance from within our cellular structure. This inner light is released from the DNA, which mutates due to the very high frequencies. It is this mutation that leads to higher states.

Superabundance takes this process a step further. The light streaming forth from within goes on expanding, and as it does, it reaches out into the environment and touches the space and the objects around it. The light of consciousness impregnates and quickens anything or anyone nearby. Next to such an energy, your DNA begins to mutate through resonance. If someone isn't ready for this kind of transformation, they will simply leave. They will find their reason to escape, or else life will do it for them.

You see this phenomenon around all great beings of light – the great teachers. The light enters the lives of the disciples, and of anyone who even thinks of the teacher or the guru and holds them dear to their hearts. It reminds me of the woman who touched the hem of Jesus's cloak, thinking he didn't know – and was transformed by her faith.

This is called the grace of the guru. It isn't hampered by time or space. The guru or being of light need not even be still living. The superabundant nature of the divine consciousness goes on growing and expanding down the ages – we just need to tap into it.

Sri Anandamayi Ma, the great Indian saint said of those who were drawn to her:

> *One who has once been attracted to this body, even though he may make a thousand attempts, will not be able to efface or blot out the memory. It will remain and persist in his memory for all time.*

She is not talking about her physical body here, but the divine impulse animating it: the Light.

Remember these four Pillars. They are the foundation of this entire teaching – Beauty, Unity, Truth, and Illumination – the four primary words for love.

The Fourth Dare

Part 2

The Second Four Dares

Solve Et Coagula

DARE TO BE DIVINE

SOLVE ET COAGULA

Solve et coagula – an ancient alchemical axiom, these three words contain an entire mystic philosophy. In a nutshell, they refer to the process of alchemical dissolution in which a base metal is dissolved and destroyed and then reborn and distilled into a new substance. That new substance then goes through a series of transmutations, the result of which is the creation of gold. Thus runs the great metaphor of alchemy.

Many would say it is more than just a metaphor but that it used the actual chemical process as a means of bringing about both inner and outer transformation. Out of such alchemical experiments arose modern chemistry, through sages such as Paracelsus. From the early knowledge and practice of chemistry emerged modern medicine and healing. This is rather beautiful to bear in mind the next time you visit the doctor for some antibiotics!

Let's revisit the interior code we are using to decipher the I Ching – the nuclear hexagrams hidden inside each of the 64. When we look into these patterns, we discover the 64 can be reduced to just four hexagrams – four Gene Keys – inside all the others. I call these – the 1, the 2, the 63, and the 64 – the Four Pillars of the Temple, and the Four Pillars are Fire, Water, Truth, and Light.

The 4 Pillars of the Temple

1	2	63	64
Fire	Water	Truth	Light

Moving outwards in our pattern we find twelve additional Gene Keys. Each of these twelve is hidden inside four more Gene Keys, suggesting families or structural groupings. For example, the fifteen hexagrams and Gene Keys that fall under the 1st Gene Key make up the Pillar of Fire:

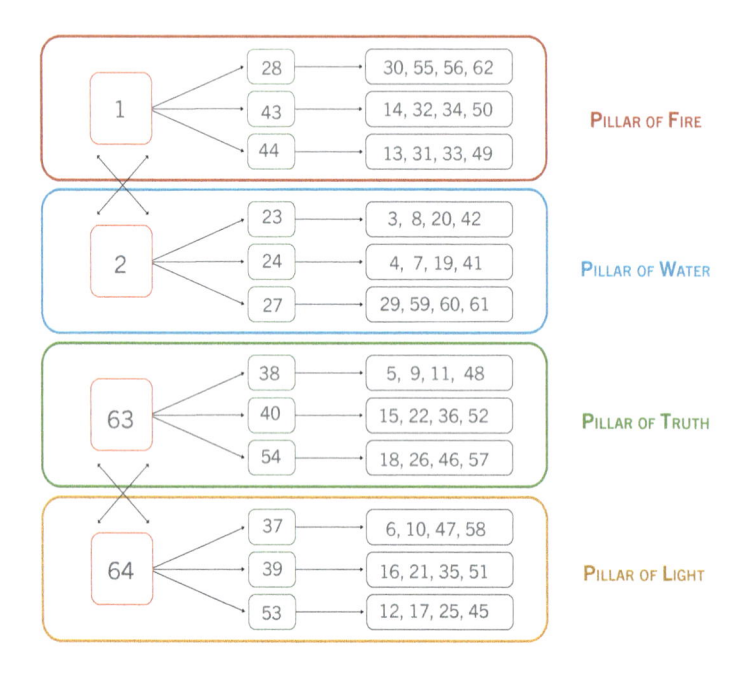

1	28 → 30, 55, 56, 62	
	43 → 14, 32, 34, 50	PILLAR OF FIRE
	44 → 13, 31, 33, 49	

2	23 → 3, 8, 20, 42	
	24 → 4, 7, 19, 41	PILLAR OF WATER
	27 → 29, 59, 60, 61	

63	38 → 5, 9, 11, 48	
	40 → 15, 22, 36, 52	PILLAR OF TRUTH
	54 → 18, 26, 46, 57	

64	37 → 6, 10, 47, 58	
	39 → 16, 21, 35, 51	PILLAR OF LIGHT
	53 → 12, 17, 25, 45	

Those grouped with the 1st Gene Key are all Siddhis of the fiery element – for even those with softer themes contain the hidden Fire.

Delving into the essence of these four Gene Key Pillars we shall start with the second layer – the 43, the 23, the 40, and the 37.

The Second Four Dares

THE FIFTH DARE — DARE TO BE DISSOLVED

We begin with the 43rd Gene Key – the Siddhi of Epiphany, and out of this Siddhi we get our first Dare – it's a wonderful dare – Dare to be Dissolved. It is rooted in the fire of the six yang lines in the 1st Gene Key, whose Siddhi is Beauty. Here we have Epiphany by Fire. Epiphany is a breaking down and a breaking through from within.

In the I Ching the 43rd hexagram is called *Breakthrough* – when we allow all our rational thinking about the world to be dissolved. Everything we believe we are knowledgeable about has to go, for the 43rd Siddhi removes all names and naming. In the fire of Epiphany, only one name survives, the name of God. Unpronounceable and unwritten, the name of God is written everywhere, in all things, over and over again. It is into this Name, this sacred *Om*, that we are asked to dissolve.

Let's take a look at the Siddhis that make up this Dare...

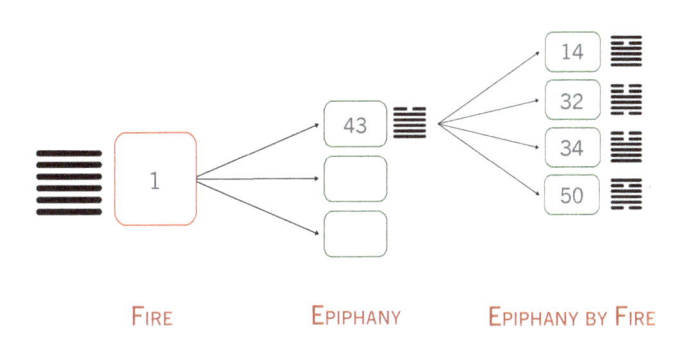

FIRE   EPIPHANY   EPIPHANY BY FIRE

THE **14** — **BOUNTEOUSNESS** — THE DISSOLUTION OF POWER

THE **32** — **VENERATION** — JACOB'S LADDER

THE **34** — **MAJESTY** — THE OLYMPIANS

THE **50** — **HARMONY** — HARMONY OF THE SPHERES

THE 14TH SIDDHI – BOUNTEOUSNESS
The Dissolution of Power

The 14th Siddhi is the very archetype of the entire aim of alchemy – gold.

In the *Crystal Alphabet*, which relates every Gene Key and line to a mineral or crystal, the 14th Gene Key represents gold itself. Here is the great symbol of our eventual glory, fire as gold, the golden apples of the sun as the poet Yeats put it.

This Siddhi emerges through self-empowerment. Gradually we learn to stop compromising our love (the Shadow of this Gene Key is Compromise) and open into the splendour that lies in our breasts, in our hearts. We discover our core competencies in life, those things that emerge from our hearts in service to the whole.

But this Siddhi takes us to a whole other level, for the 14th Siddhi is one of the miracle Siddhis. You will find out the others as we go along. All the Siddhis are in one sense openings into the miraculous, but some, like this one, are deliberately showy. In this teaching, we will explore miracles in some depth, and this is a good place to begin.

Due to our materialist mindset, miracles and the miraculous are submerged in controversy. In our present culture, phenomena that cannot be proven by materialist science are dismissed as fantasy. Yet, quantum mechanics offers a case for dissolving the scientific paradigm currently held on this planet. Through dimensions beyond the human mind's capacity, the miracle transcends our frame of time and space.

Why the miraculous should occur is an open question, for one thing, the miracle greatly strengthens our faith. To be in the presence of a miracle is to enjoy some karmic good fortune. To witness a miracle is to undergo an utter transformation.

Apart from nature's everyday miracles such as the sunrise and springtide, I speak here of paranormal miracles which defy our limited logic of time and space. Neither am I referring to the magic tricks done by conjurors on TV.

Years ago, when I was in London, I met a man who some called the Wizard. He had mastered a deep self-hypnotic technique. At a dinner party he was showing off, and he came to me and said, 'think of a number between 1 and 10,000 and hold it in your mind.' Into my mind came immediately the number 279. He then took paper and pen, closed his eyes, scribbled, and held out the piece of paper without looking at it. On it was written 279. There was no refuting what had just happened, or of him having led me to it in an unconscious way. He just plucked it out of the field, and there it was.

The 14th Siddhi produces the miracle of materialisation. This is the ability to materialise objects out of thin air or to change one thing into another. Only a being whose heart is pure can do this. There can be no resistance in the field of your aura. If there is even a single impurity in your mind, or your emotional astral body, the signal from the higher bodies cannot be transferred to the material plane.

In fact, we all have this gift. When we display the 14th Gift of Competence we can make things happen on the material plane, but of course not instantly; it takes work and time. At the Siddhi level, however, where time and space have broken down, materialisations can be truly instantaneous.

Satya Sai Baba is an example of a miracle worker. His Sun was in the 14th Gene Key, line 6. A man surrounded by controversy (as is often the case nowadays wherever the inexplicable pops up), he was well known for materialising *vibhuti* – sacred ash – from his hands. This faculty is common among saints. It is what remains from the sacred fire that burns within a vast open heart.

SATHYA SAI BABA

You need only look at the facts of this man's life to see it... He set up 1200 centres in 126 countries, all devoted to helping people in need. You don't do that unless you feel a deep love for humanity. Nobody has to be perfect. So, discard cynical gossip and read between the lines. Some people just cannot stomach the miraculous. Others may witness something but it fries their brains and sets them on the opposite path of denial. This too is a pattern within the mystery of the miraculous. When unobstructed, however, a true miracle deeply strengthens the bonds between master and disciple and God.

Sai Baba was also known for manifesting gold objects, but I don't recommend you go and look into it. People try to discount these manifestations, and some are only interested in spreading slander. Even if they are right, they pay no attention to the man's extraordinary good deeds. We, humans, are strange indeed – you can't judge a book by its cover.

The 14th is a showy Gene Key: that gold cannot be concealed; look at this man. You're not supposed to hide this Siddhi. The original name in the I Ching is *Possession in Great Measure*!

Anything is possible when the Siddhi is reached. So the question is: what has to be dissolved? The answer is you! Your belief in separateness needs to be dissolved. Your need to have, to own, and to possess – all must be dissolved.

The Chinese symbol for this hexagram is the *Wagon Laden with Riches*; but to receive those riches you have to constantly give them away, like the Sun. This is a solar Gene Key. All its lines are yang except the 5th line, which is yin. The 5th line is traditionally the leader of the hexagram. So all your yang powers must be dissolved into the Yin in order for the mystery to work through you. Let the fires of divine love engulf you! Let them burn you into sacred ash!

The 14 also has a particular relationship to money. It is gold after all. There is no one like a 14th Gene Key to attract wealth. This is like a free inheritance – but you have to be clean and clear and have dealt with the karma.

In order to activate the 14th Siddhi inside yourself, you must allow the Divine to dissolve you because the money will come only when you are ready to give it away. Bounteousness is the giving away of everything that your heart and soul desires.

Dare to be dissolved, and let the solar fire take you into its soft, comforting breast.

THE 32ND SIDDHI – VENERATION
Jacob's Ladder

Here we have the 32nd Siddhi, another fiery epiphany – the Fire of lineage. This is a focused fire. Geometrically, 32 is half 64.

The Cabalists also loved this special number. They say there are the 32 paths to God represented by the 32 paths on the Tree of Life. Thus, this Siddhi contains all the pathways and lineages leading to the Godhead; it has also a time-travelling capacity, in particular in going backwards into the past.

Each Siddhi is an enigma. You might think that the past is past. You might think that the past is all over and done with and there's nothing we can do about it. Not so. The past is fluidic. It's changeable, just like in those time-shift movies where someone goes back in time to readjust a small event, and then the knock-on effect changes everything in the future.

The 32nd Siddhi can do that. It is the source of instantaneous healing. The 32nd Gene Key is about ancestral reverence. It can gaze deeply into your lineage and trace your roots the whole way back to an event. Then like a laser beam, the purifying fire can transmute that event at its source, freeing you for the first time from the weight of that karma. The Master draws the weight of your karma into his or her heart. He or she moves into the fire with you, for you. This Siddhi appears miraculous in the sense that it can untie knots in the souls of others.

The 32 also embraces continuity. Beholding all incarnations it can move beyond the portal of death. Like a Divine mechanic, it can tinker with the workings of karma beyond the veils of time and space.

In the Bible, there is a beautiful metaphor called Jacob's Ladder. In Jacob's dream, he sees great beings moving along and up this celestial ladder. He watches the transformation of consciousness as it moves through all beings – from the lowliest demons to the highest angels. This spectrum was caught by Dante in his *Divine Comedy* through the levels and layers of *Inferno*, *Purgatorio*, and *Paradiso*.

The ancestral lines behind us support our ascent, as we support those who will follow us. We are all of us in this game together. We incarnate and do a few good deeds, which make it possible for the next being to step further. Then we return, and those before us have made it easier for us. Veneration takes place at every rung of the ladder.

The 32 can see right down your lineage or fractal line. It can smell you. It knows who you were and who you will be. It deeply honours and venerates the chain of life, while seeing through the illusion of death. The knowledge and wisdom that it carries can open you up. This is a wisdom key – the transformative fire of wisdom. When the Master gives you a small epiphany – recognition beyond death of who you are or were, or clarity with some karmic working in your life, which allows you finally to let go – that is the fire of the 32nd Siddhi at work. And one final thing – this is about the blessings of the lineage. Spiritual lineage builds up a field of blessing. The goodwill down the ages – of those masters, saints, and students. Their spiritual practices and prayers have built a living field on the higher causal plane. Anyone can take advantage of this field of blessing.

The moment you honour and revere the lineage, all its blessings are yours – they surround and protect you, particularly as you move through the cycle of death and rebirth. This is the purpose of the great death/rebirth teachings, for example in the Tibetan *Bardo Thodol*, the Book of the Dead – the teachings assure that you will take a fortunate rebirth.

Those who died have not really died. The great Masters are alive on the higher planes and can be directly tapped into at any time. Not many people realise this. It is believed that you must have a living Master on the physical plane, but a Master on the subtle plane can be equally transformative. The experience is more subtle and requires deeper faith. This is often the path of advanced disciples – to forge alliances with beings beyond the veil.

These are the mysteries of the 32nd Siddhi, the veneration of the lineage. What you are dissolved into is not the Master himself or herself, but the luminous lineage behind them.

Dare to be dissolved in the blessings of the lineage or lineages that you feel most strongly aligned with.

THE 34TH SIDDHI – MAJESTY
The Olympians

Like the 32nd Siddhi, the 34th Siddhi also takes us right back to the past, but in a different way. It takes us into our animal past, into our physical roots.

This is about enlightenment through movement; through physical posture, dance, yoga, martial arts, or gesture. This is the opposite of the 52nd Siddhi of Stillness.

Consider Patanjali, the great sage of ancient India. The Divine fire came into his body and started forming spontaneous postures – *Asanas* – the breathing patterns that are hidden deep within our cellular structure.

The universe is contained in our bodies. Each posture in Hatha Yoga is related to an animal or bird or insect and we can tap the essential power of that creature.

It's the same in martial arts. The founder of aikido – Morihei Ueshiba, caught the Siddhi of Majesty through flow. He discovered the way divine fire flows like a river of love whose only desire is to bring reconciliation. All aggressive forces are neutralised and reconciled in the noble art of aikido.

Consider also the celebrated sportsmen and women throughout history. How does your contemporary sports icon rise to that level of mastery? Through persistence yes, but also through grace. Where did that persistence come from? The 34th Siddhi brings a taste or a memory of the higher state through focused movement. The greatest sportsmen and women speak unanimously of this state – the gamma brainwave where the ego ceases to be, the mind is quiet and all that remains is the flow of the movement itself.

That flow is strength. We humans have always revered our heroes and heroines, whether in sport or battle. We seek perfection – the perfection of the Godhead within each of us.

Whenever we capture a glimpse of that Majesty in motion, it reminds us unconsciously of who we truly are.

The 34th Siddhi will always break new ground. It will invent a new sequence of movements in some way, unlocking a fresh aspect of the hologram as it moves through the body. This may manifest in many fields from the arts and sciences to the humanities. The essence is perfection and grace in movement; a direct transmission of the enlightened state. Allow yourself therefore in any physical gesture or dance, to be dissolved in the movement itself.

Movement is fire in action. The epiphany arises through the body when a god or an angelic being is allowed to enter into you. As it takes over, thus your resistance dissolves.

I experienced this once when taking magic mushrooms as a young man. I found myself walking with zero tension. I sat inside my body and the body walked, with myself utterly at rest within it. I can't explain the blissfulness of that feeling – it was like riding an elephant. This is where the 34th Gene Key is taking us as a species – to the peak of our physical potential.

We aren't here to escape into the clouds. We are here to bring the higher dimensions into the physical form – into the temple of our body. One day our bodies will perform superhuman feats like those we see in our fantasy tales. I leave you to ponder the magic and mystery of the 34th Siddhi.

Dare to be dissolved into this majesty that we each hold within our bodies...

THE 50TH SIDDHI – HARMONY
Harmony of the Spheres

This one is a beauty! The true Masters – and those are rare – have manifested their higher bodies right down into the three lower realms: the physical, astral, and mental –

where we humans currently live. We may get flashes of the higher realms if we are on a spiritual path, but still, we have to integrate those into the denser medium of our lower bodies.

After a retreat or a life-changing spiritual insight, we often go through a period of integrating the emerging paradigm into our mental and emotional life, and finally into our physical body and cellular memory. The Masters have already assimilated the whole package. They're continually integrating higher harmonies and frequencies into the physical world. The resonant field of these higher frequencies becomes hugely powerful on the lower planes. This is referred to as the Master's field of grace. The grace in that presence opens us up to higher harmonies. Being in the presence of a Master will reframe your reality. It will reorganise your emotional body and it may put your physical body through the transformational fires.

Like a Divine tuning fork, the 50th Siddhi contains the musical secrets of the universe. When you approach this energy you begin to receive and vibrate to that harmonic – for the entire universe is musical. Not only that, but when you are perfectly attuned, everything to which you are connected resonates. Everyone close to you is affected by that grace. The Master's fractal field extends far beyond their physical location. It is contagious.

There are many examples of this. Some good ones come from the life of Peter Deunov, a great teacher from Bulgaria. I have a book written shortly after he died by one of his disciples who collected as many stories about him as he could. Whatever the problem a disciple might bring – a friend in need or a member of their family who happened to be sick – the Master would attend to it. He might give some instruction like, 'Take a flower and give it to them three times in a day in a glass of water'. Whatever it was didn't matter; the next day they would be better.

The physical action carried by the disciple was semi-symbolic. The Master's thought would be transferred to the dying or sick person and the harmony and grace moved there through the lineage connection. How can our minds comprehend that vast precision?

This next short sweet story has a simple beauty. I think it opens us up to the harmonic field and how far it extends.

One day in the middle of a dharma talk, Peter Deunov paused for no apparent reason, closed his eyes, and became silent. All eyes were on him. After a minute or two, he opened his eyes and continued his talk as though nothing had happened. Later that day one of his students asked him why he had fallen silent. He replied:

> *I discovered a sheep swimming to an island across the sea, and it had got lost and was swimming out to sea. It was going to drown, so I spoke to it and turned it around and I guided it safely to land.*

Isn't that beautiful? These stories open up the great possibilities of the inner world.

PETER DEUNOV

Everything in the cosmos is connected through this higher web – the harmony of the spheres. In our ultimate subtle body, the monadic body, we have never left this unity nor can we ever leave it. On our journey of return, the currents of involution and evolution come to meet each other and recreate this harmony on the physical plane. This is why we are here in these bodies – to bring the revelation into the world.

Music wonderfully symbolises the entire process because as our ears recognise the harmony, so our spirit follows, and we are drawn into the Presence. Discover your own Divine tuning fork.

Dare to dissolve the idea that you are separate into the higher frequencies you are approaching. Let the fires of the firmament purify your heart, body, and soul. Ally yourself to the Master – it doesn't matter which one – and gradually you will hear the music in your inner ears, in your cells, and the core of your human heart. Dare to be dissolved in the epiphany.

The Harmony of the Spheres

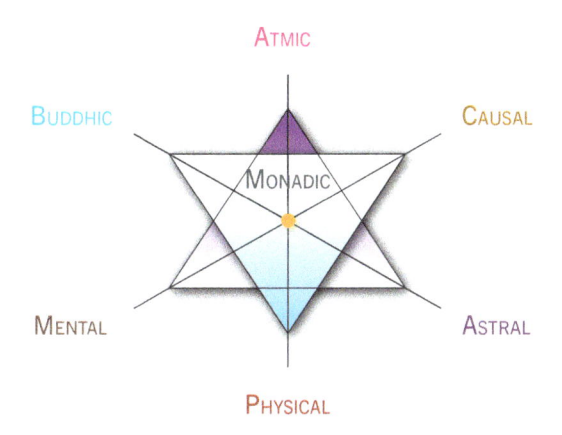

- Atmic
- Buddhic
- Causal
- Monadic
- Mental
- Astral
- Physical

The Seven Bodies in their Involution and Evolution Triads

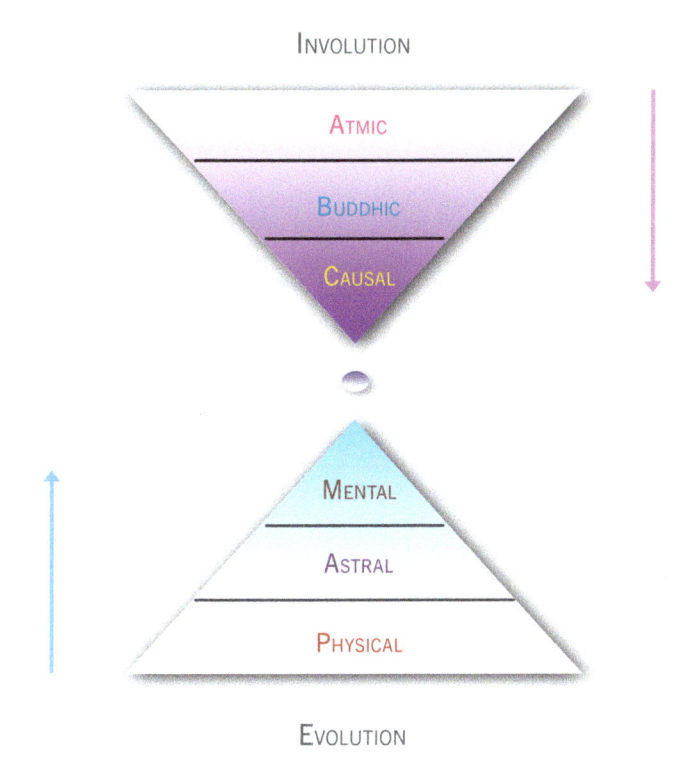

Involution

- Atmic
- Buddhic
- Causal

- Mental
- Astral
- Physical

Evolution

THE SIXTH DARE — DARE TO SURRENDER

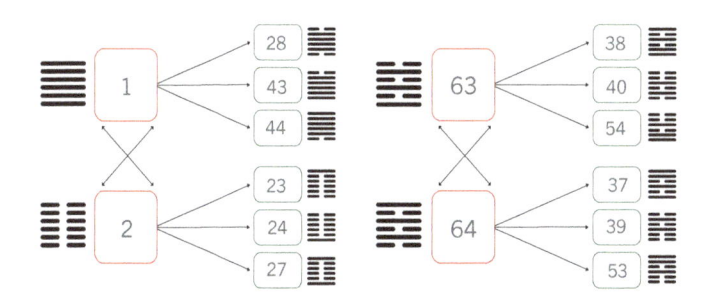

```
      ┌─ 28                    ┌─ 38
  1 ──┼─ 43                63 ─┼─ 40
   ╲  └─ 44                 ╲  └─ 54
    ╲ ┌─ 23                  ╲ ┌─ 37
  2 ──┼─ 24                64 ─┼─ 39
      └─ 27                    └─ 53
```

Solve et coagula – we've had Fire, now we come to Water. This is alchemy – fire dissolves, whereas water softens and rounds the edges of all it touches.

An entire Mystery philosophy is contained in these two words. *Solve* refers to a process of dissolution, as we let life humble us over and over again. *Solve* reaches our suffering directly. Whatever is most challenging in your life right now, that is where *solve* is most needed. *Solve* invites you to let go, to move through a transformation, to let yourself be burned in the refining fire of love. We will look at *coagula* later on.

We look now into the sixth dare – Dare to Surrender. Surrender is another aspect of *solve* because we have to be brought to our knees. We have to learn to surrender to the present moment and all its challenges.

Having dissolved into the fires of love and suffering, we now surrender into the waters of the unknown to discover our deepest essence. The deep quintessence is always something beautifully simple – this is no flood – it is a mere droplet.

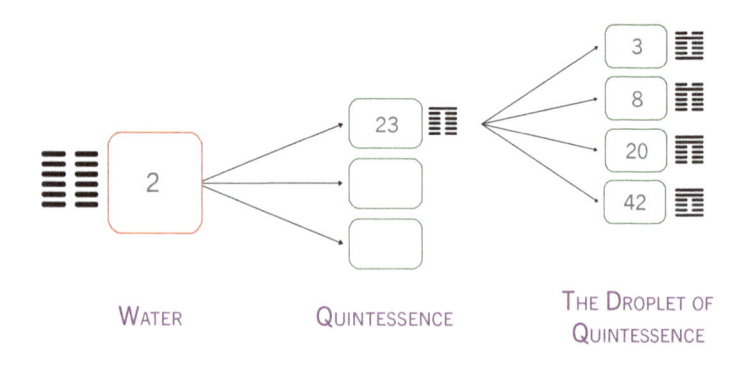

```
          WATER              QUINTESSENCE         THE DROPLET OF
                                                   QUINTESSENCE
```

THE 3 – **INNOCENCE** – SURRENDERING TO CHANGE

THE 8 – **EXQUISITENESS** – SURRENDERING YOUR SELF-IMAGE

THE 20 – **PRESENCE** – SURRENDERING TO THE NOW

THE 42 – **CELEBRATION** – SURRENDERING TO DEATH

The 23rd Gene Key holds the master code for all the Gene Keys that make up this sixth Dare. Each one is a doorway into our Quintessence.

It is also through the 23rd Siddhi that we enter the mystical Pillar of Water – held by the 2nd Gene Key of Unity. Before discovering Unity, we must unlock our uniqueness – our Quintessence.

What follows are the four lessons of surrender (the 3rd, 8th, 20th, and 42nd Gene Keys) we must pass through in order to unlock our Quintessence.

THE 3RD SIDDHI – INNOCENCE
Surrendering to Change

The journey begins with Innocence. The 3rd Gene Key governs all archetypal cellular cycles on our planet. All human beings move through natural seven-year cycles. Our birth begins this process. But our initial innocence contains a tiny flaw that starts to grow in our first seven years. This is described in depth in the Venus Sequence – which shows us precisely how the world wound becomes personalised. Thus we each fall from Grace, leaving the Garden of Eden and losing our innocence. Every parent knows this – how each child slowly loses touch with their natural state of innocence. It's a bittersweet process.

The 3rd Siddhi, however, has rediscovered its innocence. It has arrived back at the other end of its human evolution. It has travelled all the way back to its source and unlocked its unique creative quintessence.

No matter what happens to us in our lives, no matter what our karma is, we never utterly lose the innocence in our hearts. No matter how deeply an individual may embrace evil or chaos, this pure inner being cannot be shaken off. It sits eternally within our core. It may be utterly obscured, but those in whom the 3rd Siddhi is active can unlock it in a second. They can reach into any being and instantly touch the Innocence of their heart.

This is a Siddhi that can therefore create sudden awakenings or sudden conversions, but it does so with no agenda. The 3rd Siddhi is childlike, but it has the wisdom of an ancient *rishi*, an ancient being. Imagine that – to have the heart of a child coupled with the mind of a Buddha. That's you! And this tiny droplet of distilled love abides within each of us.

The theme throughout the 3rd Gene Key is change. We cannot escape this change. Change is all there is. But it takes a childlike heart to embrace this perpetual change. To approach the siddhic state, you have to have the heart of a child. You have to be deadly earnest, but you also have to be seriously playful. These are the playful masters. They are soft-hearted like children. They can melt you with their delight and with their mischief.

BABI HARI DASS

I met Baba Hari Dass when I was teaching a few years back in the USA – we used his retreat centre for a big course. I don't know his birth data, but he had this childlike manner and smile. He was one of these playful Masters. He took a vow of silence when he was quite young, and he hadn't spoken since the 1950s. He sat in a big chair with hollow arms, and inside it, he kept a little squirrel – a child's glove puppet – and as we sat there talking to him, (he responded by writing on a slate) he suddenly surprised us all by bringing out the little squirrel from inside his chair, with his hand inside it. He was moving it around and laughing with us. It was hilarious – a surreal, beautiful moment.

But he also had another side. I recall one person asking him the question: 'What have you learned from your silence?' He wrote on his slate in response, the simple words: 'that nothing is real.' Then suddenly for a moment, he looked deadly serious. It was beautiful. So that is the 3rd Siddhi – Innocence – the Quintessence of Unity.

Dare to surrender to the child within you.

THE 8TH SIDDHI – EXQUISITENESS
Surrendering your Self-Image

Dare to surrender your self-image. The Siddhi cannot imitate. You will never see two Christs or two Kabirs or two Milarepas. The Siddhi's expression is ever new, always unique. This is the essence of Exquisiteness.

Along our timeless journey to truth, we have to surrender many things, and one of the biggest is our self-image – what many refer to as the *ego*. I prefer the term self-image because your ego is your more fundamental sense of *I*. The *I* remains and becomes one vast *I*. What you do let go of is your little *I* – the one that thinks *I* have any control, any power of my own, or even any ownership of *my self*.

One thing that happens in a siddhic state is that you lose all sense of privacy. You become an open book for the cosmos to flow through you, because *you* aren't there. You have given up all attempts to hold on. The name of this hexagram, funnily enough, is *Holding Together* – some old Taoist joke, I guess. This Siddhi is unable to hold on to anything! You have to embrace the chaos by letting it all fall apart – your past, your memories, your sense of personality, your tastes, everything familiar which substantiates the illusion of your separateness.

You even have to surrender your privacy. That's a good one for us all in this modern age of the individual rebel.

This is solve et coagula – you, first of all, have to be dissolved in order for the new you, the real you, to be reborn.

We have already looked at the 14th Siddhi – The Golden Apples of the Sun. Here in the 8th Siddhi, its programming partner, we have The Silver Apples of the Moon – that is, the exquisite depth of the feminine.

This is a Siddhi that is developed particularly in the female form. You don't have to be born a woman, but it may be more commonplace if you are. A woman (or man) expressing this Siddhi is bewitching. This is the lunar light – the elfin light of the stars – a quintessence not of this world.

This exquisiteness may also emerge as genius in the present moment. Milarepa, the great Tibetan Master sang out thousands upon thousands of exquisite poems. They poured from his heart in an endless torrent, each word a glittering diamond.

The 8th Siddhi breaks you apart through the power of her voice. Each word, sound, or tone is a diamond cutting through your aura and your conditioning to hit your essence. She will go on bombarding your essence with her sonorous, siren song until you no longer think about who you are. No one hearing such a song can resist.

If you have the 8th Gene Key in your Profile or you feel deeply drawn to this Siddhi, try this out: just let your pure heart speak.

It's not as easy as it sounds, but if you manage it, you will catch a fragment of what you are capable of when you have utterly surrendered the trappings of your lower self, when you've let go of your time-saturated ideas of death and birth, of self and other, of right and wrong.

Dare to be exquisite. Dare to surrender your precious self-image and let go into eternity.

THE 20TH SIDDHI – PRESENCE
Surrendering to the Now

One of the most mystical and yet mundane of all Gene Keys, the 20th Gene Key conveys a wonderful sense of divine ordinariness. Because of this ordinariness, this is a Siddhi that can remain deeply hidden from view.

There are Masters in the world who go unseen. There have always been such people among us. Only those with the eyes to see will be able to receive them. We might also think some of them a bit strange, or perhaps even mad, but they are here nonetheless.

When I lived in New York many years ago, during a very mystic cycle of my life, I had a very fated encounter with this Siddhi. At that time I had no responsibilities, and I was being taught the mysteries by an urban shaman. We used to go to a cafe together for breakfast, and there was this old man in there who would always look around and beam this big, beautiful smile at all the people in the cafe. He was very old, but very radiant, as though his skin were shining. After a while, everyone just got used to him. He was also a perfect gentleman with old-school manners. Anyway, one day we got talking. I don't recall the conversation itself, but I do recall something he said: he told me he was 120 years old. That got my attention. And looking at him, you know, I totally believed him. There was something undefinable about him – he seemed ageless. I only remembered him today while tuning into this Siddhi. Maybe that's why I met him – so that one day I would have a human reference point for this 20th Siddhi – the simple human radiance of Presence.

This Siddhi stands apart from all the others. It stands behind all the others in a mystical way. It's the only word for any of the Siddhis with the prefix 'The'. We don't always print it so, but it should be The Presence.

As we open up into the highest states of consciousness, the Presence begins to dawn within us, spreading to every cell of our being. We become saturated by the Presence. You can never forget your car keys again after the Presence has come to live in you. It is so deep that nothing is overlooked. It is the end of all distractions. There is nothing but this overflowing awareness.

We've seen the 34th Siddhi of Majesty. And it's only majestic because of this Presence. In the same way, the 1st Siddhi is beautiful because of this Presence, and the 42nd Siddhi can only celebrate because of the Presence. It's the same with every Siddhi. Our every micro-movement is known and imbued with the Presence. One cannot even fall asleep anymore. Even if the body sleeps, the Presence continues unbroken. You hear stories of great Masters who no longer need to sleep. The Presence replenishes the body's vitality, and nothing is wasted anymore. There are no energy leakages within our being.

So what then of the past and the future? They are gathered in the present. The past and the future are enlivened in the present. They are not lost or forgotten. That's not the correct way of seeing Presence. The past is known. The future is known. You can only be fully present when you see it all. With Presence comes absolute knowledge. This is omnipresence. It's a difficult concept for the dualistic mind to imagine. To know your future? To be aware of every detail, not as a sequence, but with your memory working simultaneously backwards and forwards. There is no longer any uncertainty in your cells.

You are breathed by God. In this Siddhi is the Divine breath. This is the ultimate state. In order for this Siddhi to manifest fully, a rare event must occur. This is an avatar Siddhi, and an avatar is a descent of Grace into the form, and it generally only comes at turning points in human evolution. This is the logoic plane, a dimension beyond any conceptualisation.

This is the mythical 8th body – the logos. There are no other levels beyond this. Everything dissolves back into the wormhole. The 20th Siddhi is like a black hole – it sucks in thoughts, words, symbols – it even sucks in meaning. It is the very breath of the beyond. It is the Holy Aum – the very breath of God. What else can I say?

THE 42ND SIDDHI – CELEBRATION
Surrendering To Death

Remember, these four Keys all lie within the coils of the 23rd Gene Key – the Quintessence. This is solve et coagula; dissolve in order to be reconstituted.

The 42nd Gene Key is about dying. You can see the theme here, dissolving, surrendering, dying. Surrendering to death is not what it may seem. It is not just about giving up. Death is a fact of life. In this teaching, we are laying out the future consciousness of humanity. A deep part of that is about preparing our minds for the miraculous.

As I have travelled further into these contemplations, moments have arisen in which things have come through my higher intuition and completely surprised me! Contemplating the 42nd Siddhi brought me to an amazing notion. I already know, in my bones, that anything is possible in this universe. That is the foundation of the siddhic state. I also know that many others have come before me and have already unlocked these secrets. One of these secrets is about sidestepping death. Surrendering utterly to death means that you also transcend death. Because whatever you surrender to, you eventually transcend.

I discovered intuitively through my cellular memory, that in this world there are people who have done this. I don't think there are many. There are people among us today who have been awake for centuries, perhaps even millennia.

This seems to be the stuff of fantasy, but as I said, the Siddhis open our minds up to the seemingly impossible.

Imagine this – you have found the Quintessence! You have found that mysterious substance, the philosopher's stone, the water of life. It's a substance that can be produced by ultra-subtle hormones within the body. It is the subtlest of the subtle, the tiniest distillation of all that is purest in us, and just the minutest drop will grant immortality.

People have discovered this at certain times in history. Imagine for yourself if you were one, whom could you tell? Maybe one or two trusted friends, but they would be the type of people who would keep the secret.

I have been wondering about this for myself – what would I do with all those centuries of life? If it were me, if I had more time, I would study, I would travel, I would explore. I would learn all languages, I would learn all skills. I would talk to all people and be of the whole world, while ever at work to refine and polish my inner consciousness.

In a way, dying and reincarnating are very inconvenient… It all must be relearned each time. With the philosopher's stone, we go on and on absorbing the eternal life, the Presence. This feeling welled up in me as I was contemplating this Siddhi, so I just want to drop its seed here for you to contemplate yourself.

The 42nd Gene Key Siddhi is also about celebration. This contemplation bore its fruit for me. I was deep inside the 42nd Gene Key, letting it move through my inner life in its own way. As I contemplated it, at times it would drop away, and I would do some ordinary things again. Then it would come back up to the surface again. One day as I was in this reverie, wondering: 'God, these people, where are they now? Are they even aware that I am thinking of them and talking about them right now?' – just at that very moment, a song came on the radio – an amazing song recorded by the band Queen, *Who Wants to Live Forever?* from the film *Highlander*, and it's about the immortals who live concealed among us. It was a nice moment – a kind of confirmation of the truth of the philosopher's stone.

Above all, we are here to celebrate the mystery of living and dying. If I had thousands of years I would do just that. In the *Pearl Sequence* of *The Golden Path*, Celebration is the 3rd line keynote of the Pearl itself. It's one of the six Pillars of Prosperity – to love and learn, to be human, to dance, to share, to feast on life, and of course to let go: that is the 3rd line. When you love someone and they die, you have to let them go. But when you enter into the true nature of death you see the nature of its illusion – that only the shell dies. Every human being since the dawn of time has carried this deep intuitive knowing about the illusion of death.

The reason is that once upon a time, long ago, we lived in a more merged field of consciousness where the truth was known directly. There is a soul, there is a mid-being that lives on in a body made of light – of Quintessence. That part of us lives through all these lives until one day all the souls return to the ocean of life, to the great source. But until that day, even the soul has to evolve. It is the most astonishing story ever conceived, and the 42nd Gene Key contains the full story, including the happy ending: and they all lived happily ever after. That's this Gene Key. So let that sink deeply into your cells.

All will be well, and all is well. This Truth will bring you so deeply into the moment that you will even forget there is a story. Dare to surrender to your inevitable transcendence of death. One day you will remember these words. One day you will recall this feeling. One day...

So, we have looked at the Pillars of Fire and Water – the alchemical elements that must be mystically combined and recombined to produce the Quintessence and the Epiphany. Now we move from *solve* to *coagula*. Coagula, as the word and its sound suggests, is about something appearing from nothing. It's about the crystallisation of consciousness into truth and light.

THE 4 PILLARS OF THE TEMPLE

1	2	63	64
FIRE	WATER	TRUTH	LIGHT

THE SEVENTH DARE – DARE TO BE DECISIVE

We have seen the 43/23 axis. This is the Axis of Dissolution. Now we have the 40/37 axis. This is the Axis of Reconstitution. These are the axial planes in the great wheel of life. If you know Human Design, you will recognise them. They appear in many people's Profiles. The 40 and 37 as programming partners are about building and reforming and combining.

Let's just go back for a moment to consider the 63rd Siddhi, out of which this 40th Gene Key is born. The 63rd is the Gene Key of Truth. And what is truth?

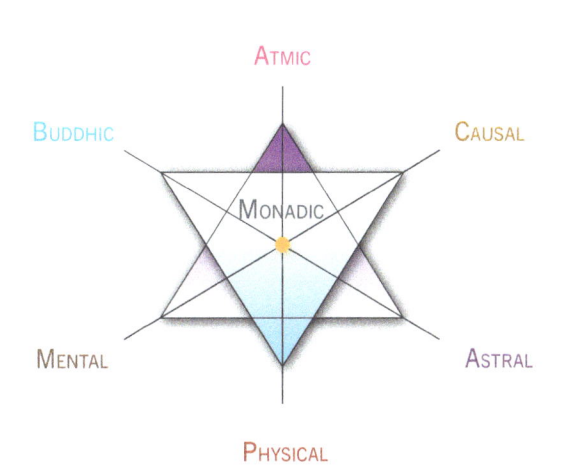

THE HARMONY OF THE SPHERES

ATMIC

BUDDHIC   CAUSAL

MONADIC

MENTAL   ASTRAL

PHYSICAL

Here are the subtle planes or bodies of the full human being. The seventh one, the Monadic, is inside them all. There is a lower trinity and a higher trinity. Our vision through the mind is limited; living in the realm of matter, we sense through the physical dimension, we feel through the astral/emotional dimension and then we think through the mental field.

At this current stage in our evolution, we are not generally aware of the upper dimensions because we have fallen and forgotten our true nature. This is why we have all the seeking, and hence the current of evolution, the force, the pressure to come back to wholeness.

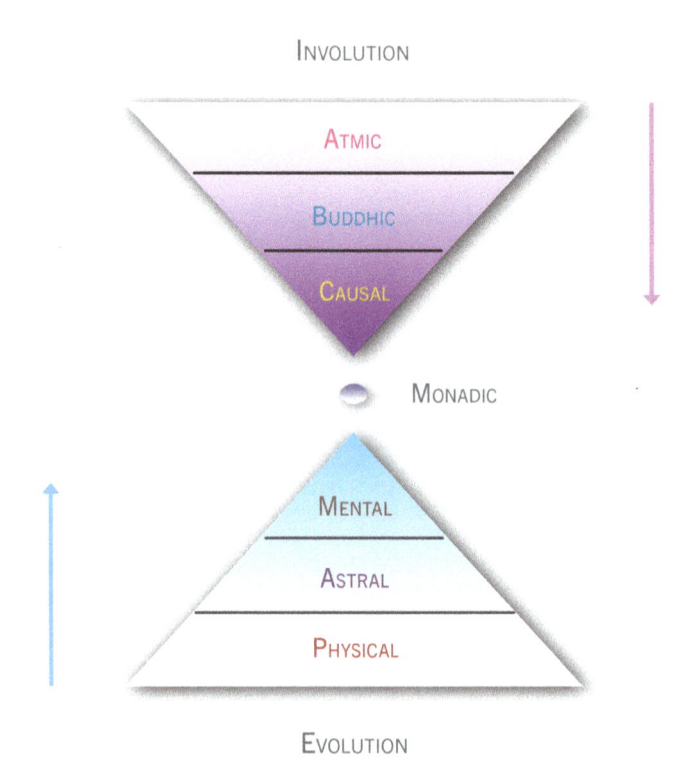

INVOLUTION

ATMIC

BUDDHIC

CAUSAL

MONADIC

MENTAL

ASTRAL

PHYSICAL

EVOLUTION

In the upper trinity, we find the causal, buddhic, and atmic bodies, in which consciousness is refined and broadened progressively as we ascend the ladder of frequencies. On the causal plane, we find wisdom, where all things are known in the holographic cosmic pattern. This, the plane of pure genius triggers all our great human mental breakthroughs.

Then we have the buddhic plane – the plane of cosmic love. This is the higher arc of the astral plane where love exists but is purified of desire. This is unconditional love, pure love. This plane is accessed only rarely by the ecstatics and saints of this world.

Finally, we come to the atmic plane, the dimension of Truth. Truth is higher even than love and wisdom, because – in my definition – Truth is the fusing of love and wisdom. Truth is beyond words. The atmic plane knows no words. The descending current of involution is also seeking wholeness. This is the pressure of the Divine to become integrated into the form principle.

The 63rd Gene Key, representing this Pillar of Truth, is a deep, transcendent science. The 64 is art, the 63 is science. At the higher level, this is a different kind of science – this is Divine science. This is our future science, as was always taught in the Mystery Schools. This is the science of synthesis. It combines the objective scientific method with subjective mystical discovery. Both hemispheres of the brain work together. This is our future science.

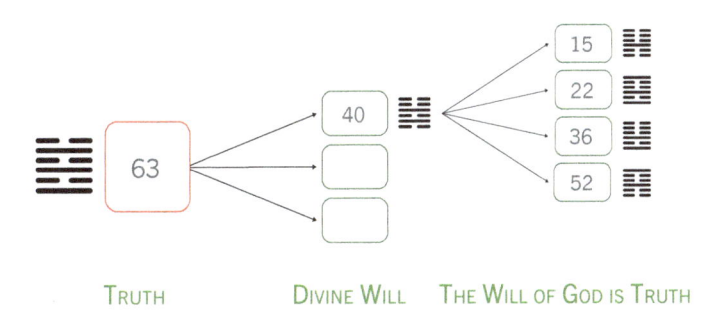

TRUTH   DIVINE WILL   THE WILL OF GOD IS TRUTH

THE 15 – **FLORESCENCE** – LOVE THY NEIGHBOUR AS THYSELF

THE 22 – **GRACE** – THE DESCENT OF THE DOVE

THE 36 – **COMPASSION** – THE DARK NIGHT OF THE SOUL

THE 52 – **STILLNESS** – THE STILL POINT

So, consider again the 40th Siddhi – we have Truth and Divine Will. This Pillar of Truth is intense. It is about being inwardly strong. This is Dare to be Decisive. This is the sword of Truth. Here we need to make a powerful commitment.

To attain the highest, we must first surrender to the will of the whole, and then allow that will to work in us. That gives us a serious Resolve – the Gift of the 40th Gene Key. But Divine Will is a mysterious Siddhi, as we shall see from the four Siddhi's that it gives birth to.

THE 15TH SIDDHI – FLORESCENCE
Love thy Neighbour as Thyself

We begin with the 15th Siddhi – Florescence; a wonderful word and a wondrous Siddhi.

These people can touch anything and it sprouts back to life. When Jesus brought Lazarus back to life, it may have been through this life-giving Siddhi. Florescence is the power of the green, the power of nature, the power of life's vitality to grow and flower and blossom and fruit.

The 15th Siddhi seeks out the deserts. It deliberately seeks out the dry and the dead. And it brings life back to those places, to those parched people and dying creatures. Think about this role of the 15th Siddhi if you have it in your Profile, or if you are mysteriously drawn to it. These Siddhis transcend all individual Profiles.

Once the inner decision is made to serve God, to serve the will of the whole, to make love the centre of our life, God begins to sprout in our life.

Decision is actually the mystical name for one of the initiations – we each have to make this great decision at some point in our evolution. Once it is made, our life changes irrevocably. To love thy neighbour as thyself is the decision to put love above all else – not in a self-obsessed way, but as pure love – love as service, love as philanthropy, love as Truth. Love as Truth brings us, humans, closer together.

The 40th Siddhi is a lone force. Only you can make the decision. It's made deep inside your aloneness, but once it's made, it paradoxically brings you together with others who have also made the Great Decision.

Coagula forges links and bridges. Coagula unites us. Only those who have a strong inner aloneness really know how to work together. If you fear the group, if you fear the tribe or community, perhaps your aloneness isn't yet strong enough. If your aloneness were strong enough, you wouldn't fear it might be compromised.

Out of this decisive love flows all manner of fruits and gifts. One level of the 15th Siddhi is in the individual. You become a polymath – your gifts flower across multiple fields in multiple dimensions. There's nothing you can't turn your hand to. There is no one to whom you won't offer help. But the even greater role of this Siddhi is in bringing people together. It jumps across gene pools. It contains the secrets of group geometry. It unites the warring tribes and brings diversity into harmony.

Everyone here in Europe right now is concerned about the splitting apart of the European Union, and about the divisive nationalistic movements around the globe. But I can tell you that in the end, it may work out for the good. It's all up to the will of the whole – unity cannot be created through sameness. Centralised governing bodies cannot last. Localised governing bodies are much more healthy, but they must be networked together. Harmonic diversity then grows organically. It's very different from an imposed unification.

In harmonic diversity each group needs to retain its identity – that's its strength and its beauty. So sometimes there is a collective need to pull back and recreate or clarify those identities. Our decisiveness and strength can then bring us together in right relationship. The same principle applies to couples as it does to tribes, nations, and species. It's about respect. To respect another, we first have to build our self-respect. To love your neighbour, you must first love yourself.

This is the wonderful green and abundant world of the 15th Siddhi. It's like the goose that lays the golden eggs. Never mind the eggs – you just be the goose!

THE 22ND SIDDHI – GRACE
The Descent of the Dove

There is a great mystery in the 22nd Gene Key – the Siddhi of Grace. Grace is all-pervasive. It is a miracle Siddhi. It's the power behind all miracles. It's behind all the Siddhis. It's the favour of God. It's the reward for all your toils and travails, for your unseen acts of kindness, and your endless prayers in the middle of the night. Everything you do, think, and feel, is heard and recorded – the good and the bad. But when the good becomes strong – then the grace comes into play.

Grace has two faces. The one is the face of suffering. The deeper you commit, the more decisive your spirit becomes to keep moving inwards, transmuting the dark matter into light – the more the spirit of grace lays it on for you. She tests you and tests you. Just when you think things can't get any worse, grace pushes things that little bit further. She does this out of her infinite compassion – because we have to be broken down. We have to be brought to our knees – to have no will of our own left. We have to utterly surrender to the will of God.

Then, in the midst of our dark night, grace brings us the softest of touches, and in that instant, all our suffering is gone as we taste the peace of the one true light. The dove descends to meet us halfway. Grace brings us a boon to strengthen our faith. Whatever small miracle or gift she brings, it builds upon our faith. This is how grace works.

The other face of grace is this touch of the mother, the way she brushes the back of her hand against her sleeping child's cheek. She favours us. She loves and cradles us.

Truth is a vibration so high that we have to be prepared. To embody the power of any Siddhi we are made ready over time. The physical, astral, and mental bodies must be purified. So we are given these experiences. We are lowered into the waters of grace very slowly. If we went in too fast, our circuits would be fried. Our nervous system would not be able to handle the current.

The atmic body is beyond bliss, beyond the ecstasies of the buddhic plane, and the wisdom streams of the causal plane. When we come into contact with the face of God, all aspects of our personal self are silenced. Entering the hall of the sacred, we become one with the mystery.

This is oneness with the Divine. This experience is referred to in the 22nd Gene Key as full embodiment. Other mystical terms are realisation, enlightenment, samadhi, and the sixth initiation. If you aren't up to speed with all this, then read and re-read the 22nd Gene Key and study the *Seven Sacred Seals*. Then you will know what I am saying.

The 40th Siddhi is the first of the Sacred Seals. It represents the light of the Christ consciousness descending right down into the darkest recesses of hell. This is dare to be decisive. When you decide that serving the whole comes before all else, only then do you enter the narrow gate. Then things may become intense for you.

There are many paths to the divine. At a certain point, however, we are called inwardly to take this narrow path of the higher initiations. The lower initiations – the first four – can all take place in ordinary life. The fifth initiation, however, asks us to move into some kind of retreat. Ideally, we should be among others who can support us. The sacred and monastic communities or sanghas were formed just for this reason – so that when a member was ready for this path, the others could assist them, not only spiritually, but also physically.

But we need not worry. When that time comes for us, grace will prepare the ground. She organises everything in advance. When we are ready, she arranges our life for us to be supported as we enter the deeper reaches of consciousness.

It takes a daring soul to take full responsibility for their own suffering – to receive it graciously – to realise it is all our karma and is thus given to us as a gift. That takes a great soul, capable of vast love.

This is when the Dove – the Shekinah – the Divine Feminine, descends into our depths to lift us up to the highest.

THE 36TH SIDDHI – COMPASSION
The Dark Night of the Soul

Notice how these Siddhis flow into each other through their interconnected families. Truth is a sword. It cuts us deeply. The sword of Compassion is related to the 22nd Siddhi for the 36 and 22 are in the same codon ring – the Ring of Divinity.

Here we have the Dark Night of the Soul. Compassion is an aspect of grace. Arising out of the Gift of Humanity, it is paradoxically beyond humanity, for it comes from the stars. It is a stellar fragrance. Compassion is at the core of every atom of creation. This is what we discover as we reach right into the heart of the core wound. All the great mystics have to go through this dark night where they meet their deepest fears. This is the divine doubt of Mother Julian, a medieval mystic. We have to meet the guardian on the threshold. This is where we face the devil in the desert – our doppelgänger, our final trial. Long ago the decision was made deep inside us to come one day to this crux point. Only our valour and our light will carry us across the threshold. If we have been granted the grace of wisdom or great love, just as we reach the threshold of unity, suddenly it is all taken away, leaving us bereft and alone, in the abyss. We need that final purge so that there is nothing left in us – no subtle trace of vanity. Then our journey comes to its glorious conclusion. We enter into the mind of God.

I didn't write about what the 22nd Siddhi might do, and it's hard to say what this 36th one will do either. Their field is vast beyond our reckoning. The 22 will glow in a person through whom grace works, and so will the 36. The difference is that the 22 works with highly evolved souls, whereas the 36 works with the less evolved. The 22 puts us through intense tests before she rewards us. The 36, having gone through the realms of hell, now wishes to help others, especially those who are deeply lost.

So, the 36th Gene Key – known in the I Ching as *The Darkening of the Light* – deliberately seeks out the darkest souls and the darkest places.

There is a tradition that Christ descended into hell. It's mystically known as the Harrowing of Hell. He goes down there for three days and then he ascends again. Why does he do that? Because when you are filled with light, you are immediately drawn to the darkness. The law of light seeks out darkness; that is its great compassion. The 36th Siddhi will find the ugliest places where the most dangerous people live or the meanest demons, and it will free them.

A while ago I was drawn to a man named Bawa Muhaiyaddeen, a Master from Sri Lanka. I mentioned him in my book *The Seven Sacred Seals* as an embodiment of truth.

He came from the forests; I mean, he literally came out of the forest enlightened. No one knows who he was or anything of his story. He emerged as a Master in the Sufi tradition. And I read some of his words. He is a beautiful man. He always began his talks: 'My dearest, beautiful, sweet, loved and beloved disciples and devotees …'

Bawa Muhaiyaddeen

In one of his talks, Bawa mentioned a certain date, 15 August, sometime in the last century, when he says he vanquished 52,000 demons! You cannot understand what a Master says unless you comprehend these Siddhis. The light becomes so great that it almost needs the darkness. The light of the Siddhis is inextinguishable. The truth is irrefutable. When it faces even the darkest form of consciousness, that form has no choice but to become light. That is the will of God in action. When the Master calls, the dog comes running. It's the same with the light.

The glory of the divine is so magnificent, so resplendent, so humbling, so achingly tender and irresistible, it causes us to weep tears of release. Nothing escapes it. That is why when the mystic passes through the narrow gate, he or she becomes the bearer of good news. Never again can he or she be taken in by the old news headlines. It's all perfect. God is everywhere; existence is divine. There is nothing outside the will of Allah. All is grace, and the law of compassion stands behind everything.

The tragedies you can't make sense of in your life – why did your loved one have to die? or that innocent child? – all these things which deeply wounded you, they are all resolved when you come to this truth. I can't say how. All that grief inside us is extinguished. No one died. Everything and everyone you ever loved is alive inside your heart forever. They are all there. I mean this. I am not just talking about memories, but the quintessence of each of those you love is inside your heart, so you can never, never again lose them. This is a mystical reality.

Compassion makes us whole. After grace cuts into us, compassion makes us whole. So, dare to be decisive. Dare to relay this divine transmission into your cells, to strengthen your faith, and let it inspire you to go deeper into your spiritual practice. This is not my individual self but the transmission speaking directly to you. If you have found this teaching, it is because you are ready to hear it. Those who have ears to hear, let them hear.

THE 52ND SIDDHI – STILLNESS
The Still Point

Below is a quote from a Master, I don't know which one said it.

> *In samadhi there is only the feeling 'I am' and no thoughts.*
> *The experience 'I am' is being still.*
> *The self is God.*
> *'I am' is God.*
> *All that is required to realise the self is to be still.*

Wholeness is stillness. Truth is stillness. In the end, it stills everything. In the atmic plane, all thoughts cease. The great teachers experience and speak of the cessation of thinking. The voidness of your intellect is buddhahood.

This is from the *Glossary of Empowerment* in the *Gene Keys* book:

'The atmic plane is the sixth of the seven major planes of reality, upon which all human beings function. As the higher frequency octave of the mental plane, the atmic is the plane of your true higher self. The entire cosmos is experienced as a living mind whose primary impulse is love. When you cross the threshold to this plane through the sixth initiation, your independent thinking immediately ceases, to be replaced by pure light. To contact your greater being on the atmic plane all you need to do is consistently focus on this inner light.'

All the Siddhis that flower from within this 40th Siddhi of Divine Will are all rooted in stillness. Compassion, grace, florescence – they are all born of stillness.

Stillness is not a condition, nor is it a lack of activity or movement. It is the ground of truth. When truth dawns, then it expels all doubt from our system. No karma or attachment remains to pull our awareness this way or that. Our awareness finally comes to rest. Our whole being drinks from this deeply refreshing stillness. It's as though we have been so thirsty for so long, and then we finally find this spring inside us. It replenishes us at the deepest level.

Those beings who attain the siddhic state never really sleep. This is the Siddhi of not sleeping. The stillness is where we go at night when we sleep. Our body needs to touch the deep void, even for a few seconds. With just a few seconds of deep sleep each night, our body can revitalise itself. This stillness resets all our systems.

But when the stillness is always accessible, we can drink from it whenever we like, so sleeping is no longer necessary.

The cessation of thought is also the cessation of time. Thus we inhabit a new world. We can sit in the stillness for hours and hours and it seems only a few seconds have passed. Or we may sit in stillness for a few seconds, and years go by.

People have to take care of some of these sages because they don't live in time. Maharaji used to go out into the towns to visit his many devotees. He'd spontaneously knock on their doors at any time of day or night and be fed over and over again. One of his devotees reported that Maharaji once had over forty meals in 24 hours! The great well of stillness can absorb anything you put into it. How could he know he had eaten each time? He was just following his love.

Stillness precedes love. Love arises out of stillness, like the mist at dawn.

Touch is the final vital sense we have to let go of as the stillness fills us. In the Venus Sequence, I describe a mystical process called the Sealing of the Five Senses. Writing that section gave me chills. The first sense to develop in the womb is touch. Before all else, there is touch. The foetal movement *in utero* is our first sense that we exist. This subtlest place of identification through touch comes in the first trimester.

It is the first of the five senses to develop. A little later comes smell, as the nose develops and is saturated with the maternal smell. Then each sense comes online sequentially.

As we let go of our identification with the body, we go through that sequence in reverse. First, we let go of sight, then hearing, then taste, then smell and finally touch. And to let go of touch requires stillness. Only as we become physically still can this deepest identification drop away.

The mystics developed asanas that allow us to stay still for hours – like the lotus posture, or the zazen kneeling position in zen Buddhism. Some of the Christian mystics lay face down before the altar for hours and even days.

The stopping of physical movement in meditative absorption creates an environment in which the subtler bodies also become still. The first to fall away is physical sensation, then the astral – our states of boredom, sadness, or even joy. Finally, the subtlest of all – the mental plane – as spaciousness begins to open up between our thoughts, until one day thought ceases altogether.

From this space beyond thought, the 52nd Siddhi dawns. These Siddhis are like Russian dolls. I keep coming back to the truth that they all reside inside each other, Thus we keep returning to our Four Pillars. Stillness is truth.

Be still and know that I am God. Solve et coagula. Once the self dissolves, the true self arises. That is coagula.

Dare to be decisive. Dare to go within, no matter what, and stay on course.

The name of this hexagram is *Keeping Still Mountain*. Stay consistent and unmoving in your quest. This is the power to move mountains!

One final thing – Stillness is an inner state. You can be a whirlwind and you can be still. You can be talking and you can be still. You can be whirling like a dervish and inside you are utterly, completely in the stillness at the centre of the universe.

The Seventh Dare

THE EIGHTH DARE – DARE TO BE GENTLE

And so, we come to our final dare in the second part of this series, dare to be gentle.

The 64th Gene Key represents the Pillar of Light and the Siddhi of Illumination. Light is the foundation of creation. All matter is made of light waiting to be released and realised. This is why the 64 is called *Before Completion* because matter and the whole material world is nothing more than unrealised light that hasn't yet completed its evolution.

The 37th hexagram – called *A Gentle Wind* – also contains the nuclear hexagram 64, giving us our eighth dare. Dare to be gentle is a counterbalance to the last dare – Dare to be Decisive. Dare to be gentle is rooted in one of the great feminine Siddhis. This is the Light of the Divine Mother; the Light of Tenderness. Four other Gene Keys then have this nuclear 37 hidden inside them: the 6, the 10, the 47, and the 58.

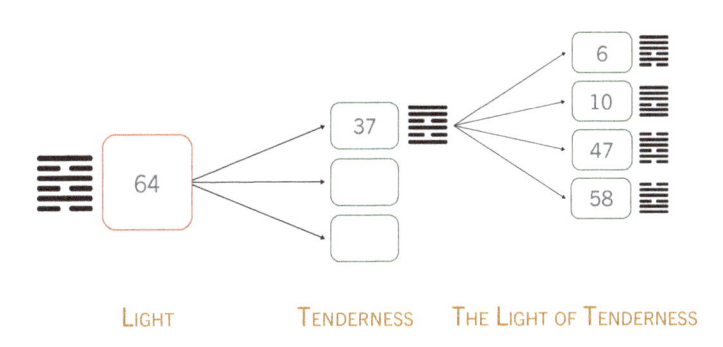

LIGHT   TENDERNESS   THE LIGHT OF TENDERNESS

THE 6 – **PEACE** – PEACE ON EARTH AND GOODWILL

THE 10 – **BEING** – SITTING BY THE RIVER

THE 47 – **TRANSFIGURATION** – KARMIC SUPERNOVA

THE 58 – **BLISS** – BLESSED ARE THE MEEK

THE 6TH SIDDHI – PEACE
Peace on Earth and Goodwill

The 6th Siddhi is a bit of a 'wow' Siddhi. This is already discussed in the Gene Keys book. It's about the body learning to live off light through the new awareness we are developing. In this sense, this is a special Gene Key for this particular time in our evolution because it holds the instructions for our future body.

The 6th Siddhi is going to rebuild the Garden of Eden. In this Pillar of Light, the future meets the past. The Garden of Eden was here at the beginning and will be here at the end, but right now we are in the middle!

Dare to be gentle reminds us that everything is okay. The Great Mother holds us in her embrace. All will be well. All is well, and this peace is a balm for our souls. It abides within the cells of each and every one of us. It's a memory signature written in light, a frequency we will one day rise into, and we each contain it.

Dare to be gentle also involves the Gift of Diplomacy. This dare is a very practical dare concerning relationships. It teaches us to bring tenderness into the many ways that we connect with each other. Emotions put us through quite a test. Peace in a relationship can only occur when at least one of the two partners manages to take full responsibility for his or her emotional state. Diplomacy isn't the same as politeness. Politeness can repress. Diplomacy feels the emotion but chooses to express it in a way that projects no personal agenda or blame. In fact with diplomacy, emotion is expressed through caring. So your love becomes a conscious choice over your reaction. That is the definition of diplomacy. If even one person does this in a relationship, suddenly the fire, the angst, and the argument are gone. If one refuses to argue, what's the other one going to do?

The Venus Sequence teaches us this subtle art of tenderness. It awakens the 6th Siddhi of Peace in each of us and shows us how to bring it into our relationships.

Perhaps you might think that this kind of peace sounds dull or somehow boring. What, no arguing? No fire or anguish and suffering? No, it is not boring. It is radical. Peace is a Siddhi – it's heaven on earth inside your body.

This is one of the Christ Siddhis. This whole group of Siddhis is Christ-centric. The infinite tenderness of the 37th Gene Key is symbolised by the lamb. This is infinite tenderness. It's Mother Mary holding the baby. Even the numbers themselves tell the story. In the Hebrew number system known as *Gematria*, 37 is a special number – it's the number of Christ consciousness.

The number six is equally unique in this way, for it is imprinted within everything in the cosmos. When you come to the Gene Keys, whichever sequence you look at, you find these six qualities of the six lines of every hexagram. The Siddhi of Peace is like this too – it's repeated everywhere in creation.

This is also one of the great Siddhis of healing. A few of the Siddhis specifically target disease. The terrific power of the healing light this Siddhi emits can bring about instantaneous healing. More than this, the 6th Siddhi contains the codes of a future medicine for humanity that is rooted in colour. The human aura is essentially a rainbow. We live on seven layers or planes, and each plane is underpinned by gradations of tone and colour. To bring the whole system into balance is like tuning the seven strings of a harp. Your chemistry can be tuned through light, sound, and diet.

This new healing science is rooted in a deep understanding of colour. Disease is perceived as an imbalance or excess of a particular colour somewhere in the aura. Once the imbalance is found, it can be specifically targeted. Where there is an excess, the opposite or complementary colour is nourished, and where there is a deficiency, the colour tone is built up and its opposite is reduced. The tones are balanced within the body by means of the pH scale, which hinges on the number seven – representing equilibrium. This is achieved by addressing diet, light, and sound. Diet is thus essentially a matter of musical frequency.

I am writing this to demonstrate how certain Siddhis contain entire transmissions which can one day assist humanity to make quantum leaps in understanding how we work. This is a leap into holism, and it's essential to the medicine of the future that the higher realms are taken into account. How could they not be?

And then as we tune our vehicle to its highest pitch, so our consciousness ripens, and the 6th Siddhi begins to radiate light through our skin. This is a hallmark of the 6th Siddhi – the translucence that can be seen and felt around a true master.

THE 10TH SIDDHI – BEING
Sitting by the River

Now we move even deeper still into these rays of light – into the 10th Siddhi – a stream of pure being. Sometimes a teaching enters the world through a hidden door. Let me tell you a story about Shirdi Sai Baba...

Once upon a time, Baba was seated in the *masjid* (mosque) with a devotee at his feet. A lizard made a tick-ticking noise, and out of curiosity, the devotee asked Baba whether the tick-tick signified anything. Was it a good sign or a bad omen? Baba replied that the lizard was overjoyed, as her sister from Aurangabad was coming to see her. The devotee sat silent, trying to make sense of Baba's words. Just then, a gentleman from Aurangabad happened to arrive on horseback to see Baba. He wanted to approach, but his horse refused as it was hungry and wanted food. He took a bag from his shoulders and threw the food in it onto the ground to remove the dirt. From inside the bag, another lizard emerged, and everybody watched her climbing up the wall. Baba asked the devotee to mark her well. She all at once strutted to her sister and after a long time of kissing and embracing each other, the two lizards danced and whirled around each other with love.

The question is: where is Shirdi and where is Aurangabad? How should the man on horseback arrive from Aurangabad with a lizard, and how could Baba foretell the meeting of the two sisters? All this is wonderful and proves the omniscience and the all-knowing nature of Baba.

SRI SAI BABA OF SHIRDI

Isn't that a wonderful little tale? This simple mystery teaches us so many things. One is that there are hidden miracles everywhere, and a whole life that goes unseen. When we enter the field of expanded consciousness we realise that everything is connected and that everything is alive with a hidden purpose and meaning, and ultimately that meaning is love.

A simple little story of two lizards makes a mockery of all our big ideas, of all our worries and concerns about the world and where it might be heading. This 10th Siddhi reminds us of the simple magic and mystery of life in front of us right here, right now.

The 10th Siddhi of Being is always linked to the notion of the *arhat*. An arhat is a being who has become enlightened but has no further interest in evolution. They are here simply to enjoy the unified state. Is that selfish? Is there enlightened selfishness? Maybe, but it's not the kind of selfishness we know. It's about being absorbed in love. It's almost as if the 10th Siddhi is our original state and it will therefore one day become our culmination.

The 10th Siddhi is unimpressed by miracles. It's unimpressed by tales of Gods or goodness or evil. It doesn't give a damn what a Siddhi is. This Siddhi of being reminds us of the basis of life – we are here to be, to enjoy, to sit by the river, and listen to the birds. We are here to BE love.

Now and then we may be lucky enough to meet someone like this – they seem to have only one setting: joy. Some grace of the 10th Siddhi may have touched them. When you have joy, you don't need to seek spirituality or enlightenment.

This Siddhi represents the simple joy of being. Its language has nothing to do and nowhere to go – it begs: why not drop all this seeking and come hang out by the river to watch the lizards? This Siddhi is a counterbalance to the more spectacular ones. The people of the 10th Siddhi are likely to go unnoticed. I mean, they will certainly be noticed, but because they don't teach, they may be regarded as simple or even defective. In fact, they are a ray of tenderness. They wouldn't harm a fly.

I love this Siddhi. If I were to play a silly child's game where you were only allowed one Siddhi, this is the one I'd choose.

It is so sweet and simple – not at all what we find in today's world. It's such a wonderful feeling to just sit with a friend without saying anything. This is the field of the 10th Siddhi. It doesn't demand silence. It doesn't demand anything. It loves to do nothing. This is a great tea-drinking Siddhi.

So contemplate this one over some tea and dare to be that gentle...

THE 47TH SIDDHI – TRANSFIGURATION
Karmic Supernova

And so we continue to move from one extreme to another – from the simplicity of being to the mystery of transfiguration.

If the 10th Siddhi is ordinary, then the 47th is *extra* ordinary. Look where tenderness leads us – it takes us the whole way. The Siddhi of Transfiguration is a Siddhi that only comes about rarely. It's different from the Siddhi of Ascension (the 54), which is earned as we evolve up the ladder of frequencies.

But the 47 is unique. It's an avatar Siddhi. The difference between an avatar and a master, broadly speaking, is that the Avatar descends to earth. The Etymology of the word comes from the Sanskrit – 'to cross over and to come down'. Avatars are also collective beings. They are emanations of divine grace (the 22) that come to earth during particular cycles and at crux points in human evolution.

There are different kinds of Avatars, but I shall talk here about one type. I call this the *stellar* avatar because it comes from another star system. This kind of Avatar descends as a spiritual hierarchy – a synarchy. It draws a veil over itself as it incarnates, and then it lives out an ordinary human life until a predestined moment of awakening. This awakening happens quickly, as in the life story of the dragonfly.

When the stellar Avatar awakens, it immediately finds itself surrounded by all the fractal aspects of its collectivity. The divine self then awakens within the Avatar, like a body awakening its limbs, to operate as a single unit.

The frequency behind the Avatar is so vast that it cannot inhabit a single body. The human vehicle in its current form could never withstand it. However, by distributing that voltage among many, it can work within the lower three worlds.

Why does the Avatar descend into embodiment? It does so for the sake of transmutation – to take on the world's karma and to accelerate the evolution of humanity.

What about the transfiguration? Well, the earthly beings at the centre of the avatar's synarchy – its nexus – only have a limited timespan. Once the awakening has occurred, they begin to ascend very quickly. After a while, they will undergo a physical transfiguration. In other words, they will pass through the Ninth Initiation into the Rainbow Body. You can read about that in the 22nd Gene Key. They cannot remain here but dissolve back into the light.

This transfiguration through the stellar Avatar is a multi-generational karmic supernova. After the initial Avatar has transfigured, the frequency reverberates over many generations and can even travel across whole cultures and continents as well.

There is an ancient tradition that thus far the avatar transfiguration has only happened to eighteen initiates. This is a significant number: two times nine.

The prime stellar avatar incarnations are patterned in trinities – that is three times three. Each avataric period can last many centuries (there have been two stellar avatar cycles so far) and in each cycle nine people were physically transfigured.

They are so rare that you can count them on your fingers – some have names that you may know – Padmasambhava (an emanation of Buddha), Jesus of Nazareth, Fu Hsi in China, (who originated the I Ching), Krishna in India (who restored the dharma), Pacal Votan in South America, Hermes Trismegistos in Egypt (Hermes Thrice Great, the father of alchemy), Merlin in Britain, Zoroaster or Zarathustra in Persia and a few more. Wherever they were transfigured, they have left a vast legacy of spiritual teachings in their wake.

So all these beings are really one singular being that incarnates through three streams or rays. According to the Gene Keys transmission, we stand at the threshold of the third of these stellar avataric incarnations. This, the final one will propel the human race into its next and penultimate stage of consciousness – the so-called sixth race. A new vehicle will evolve, and this collective incarnation will gradually transform the Earth. Furthermore, this new and third form will come as an expression of the divine feminine. It will carry the essence of the 37th Siddhi – the gentlest and most powerful of embodiments. It will affect all levels of our society and will in time bring about a transfigured humanity.

Remember solve et coagula? This is its deepest teaching. The 47th Siddhi takes on the karma of the whole and transmutes it *for* the whole. Then it recombines the elements, those shadow patterns, in a higher formula to create a new synthesis, a new humanity. It is a small wonder that the 47th Siddhi is part of the Ring of Alchemy (with the 40, the 6, and the 64). That little story should give us all something to contemplate!

Let us then see the importance of dare to be gentle. The beauty is that our gentleness is the very quality that will bring about the Great Change.

THE 58TH SIDDHI – BLISS
Blessed are the Meek

Let's travel now a bit deeper into the true meaning of gentleness...

The 37th Shadow is about weakness. Is gentleness weak? Some may believe it to be. Can you face down a tyrant with gentleness? They will laugh in your face. Look deeper. Gentleness is a spirit, a sense of being. It is benevolent. It is kind, selfless, yielding, open and it gives without question. Gentleness is the face of love. When you imagine a loving face, is it anything but gentle?

And the true power of gentleness, of tenderness, lies in its patience. It will wear anything and anyone down. There is a mystical truth in the way that an extreme condition contains its opposite. Love as gentleness will never give up on you. It will wait forever for you to open to it, the way the sun waits for the acorn to become a sapling, then finally an oak. It will coax you to your full maturity, as a mother dotes upon her child. Gentleness is as solid as a rock. It is also unyielding – it is the most indomitable force in the universe. Love as gentleness is invincible. It will not be denied. This is the power through which Christ blessed the meek. Blessed are the meek, for they shall inherit the earth – the whole Earth!

In the 58th Siddhi of Bliss is found the impulse of divine supplication – to bow before Christ, before the light, and to dedicate your entire being in service to that light – to bow in reverence and invite the light to utterly take over your life – to devote all your energy and time and precious resources to your higher purpose.

The only way the 58th Gene Key's Shadow of Dissatisfaction can be fulfilled is for it to become of service to the whole.

All avenues of potential temporal happiness must first of all be exhausted. So, we try relationships, sex, money, power, skydiving, any kind of adventure, more sex, another relationship, until finally, we come to our knees. We realise that none of these things will bring us true happiness.

Nothing brings true happiness except one thing – service. This is service to others and service to the whole – not service as a profession, not service as a business, but selfless service that comes from our heart. Each of us must come to realise that this world is not for us. It is for us to be of service to others. From out of this realisation flows the bliss.

This is the divine paradox. You give up your life and you receive the ultimate reward. The 58th Gene Key is the Gift of Vitality. So offer your precious vitality, your life force to the world, to God, and offer your life in service. There is nothing you have that is more precious to you than your life force. It is your very life.

To be meek is not to be weak. To be meek before Creation, to empty oneself of one's agenda and let the Christ light be all there is at work inside you – that's the way to beat the tyrants of this world – you wear them down. To the Christ light, a lifetime is nothing. It will gladly sacrifice its life for the higher good. It knows there is no death.

Meekness is the absolute opposite of weakness – it is the only true power. If you wish to transform someone, you cannot in any way force them. You have to kill them with kindness, as the expression goes. And you can't just do it a few times and hope it will work. It should become your whole inner philosophy. Be kind to them every single day of your life, and even that may not seem to work! But it will eventually. On some level, on a hidden plane, your love will go to work. One day, and maybe not even in this lifetime, your meekness will pay off. That soul to whom you were so kind, to whom you showed the other cheek – someday all that love will just detonate inside them – like an explosion of realisation.

In the meantime, what will happen to you? You will discover bliss. Because you have learned to give without condition, without reason, you will release unconditional love. The reward is inner Bliss. So be unrelenting in your gentleness. Treat others in this spirit, with endless patience. Two things will unfold – you will become blissful, and they will be transformed.

And of course we must, first of all, learn to be gentle with ourselves. It's no use having a gentle attitude with others and not with ourselves. That is a trick the ego plays. We need to watch out for the self-sacrificing attitude and its drama. And be forgiving with yourself. Ok, so you were naïve and you made a mistake. Feel it, learn from it, move on and let it go. It's self-indulgent to beat ourselves up. We cannot then be of full service to others or the whole.

This 58th Gene Key is the only Gene Key that has no *repressive* category at the shadow level. This is because its nature can only react. Bliss cannot be repressed – not forever. It will well up. Love cannot be repressed – it will well up. How can you repress life? It will always well up.

Look at the world today – wherever we see repression and oppression, those are forces that cannot last. The most powerful force in the universe cannot be repressed because it will never, ever leave you alone. Love will haunt you. It will stalk you. It will find you out and transform you into itself. Love is utterly ruthless. Tenderness is Truth.

Countless yogis and sages have enjoyed these blissful higher states. Love transforms us. The higher bodies reach down and lift us towards our natural state of divinity and wholeness. There is in truth nothing in the world but good news – because this force is inevitable. It is coming to us all.

The 58th Gene Key is in the Codon Ring of Seeking. We seek what we do not realise, like a blind man stumbling around in the dark. Until finally one day we discover we are seeking union, and then as we begin to climb towards God, God comes to meet us. God seeks us with equal determination. One day, the gravity of God's power becomes so strong in us that it pulls us towards and into itself and we enter into that rapture which is Bliss. And it all begins with us being gentle, like the wind.

Dare to be gentle with yourself – with others – and with the world.

PART 3

THE THIRD FOUR DARES

THE COMING OF HOMO SANCTUS

Dare To Be Divine

THE COMING OF HOMO SANCTUS

I am involved in many aspects of the Gene Keys; some are more mainstream, while others are more mystical.

In these teachings, we get to let go into the unbounded aspects of the transmission. Part two brought us towards the ocean; here we begin to dive even deeper into that ocean. We move now into the realm of prophecy – into that which has not yet occurred in our human story, into the dimension we cannot yet perceive with our physical eyes or our time-processing brain.

When we speak here of 'the future' of course, that is not true. Nothing is in the future. It is as here now as it has ever been. You are encouraged to leave your conditioned beliefs at the door. You are encouraged to dare with me, to dive deep into the field of Truth. Let your body feel the rush of the Truth as it comes through these words, these ideas, and these visions. Behind them sits the Divine.

'The Coming of Homo sanctus' is an expression taken from the 55th Gift and Siddhi, one of the Gene Keys in this next dare. *Homo sanctus* refers to 'the sacred human' that is coming. Right now, we have forgotten what we are, and we have become in a sense, godless. We live in a sleeping epoch. Even those who believe, do so through rigid religious views. We have fallen thoroughly into the material realm. Even the word God has become associated with a staid, rather dull religious way of thinking. But I tell you, God is not dull. God is scintillating.

God is behind everything and within everything. There is nothing and nowhere where God is not. These truths will return home to humanity one day. No force in heaven and earth can prevent it. It is all a matter of time. One who is anchored in Homo sanctus, in the higher dimensional field of truth, does not live confined by time. To them, time is nothing but a game. Once the game is over, you fold up the board and put it away in the box. The key then is to be a player within time, but not to forget yourself in the game.

Now, a reminder of the formula we are playing with – these are the rules of our game. The primary elements are the Pillars of Fire, Water, Truth, and Light.

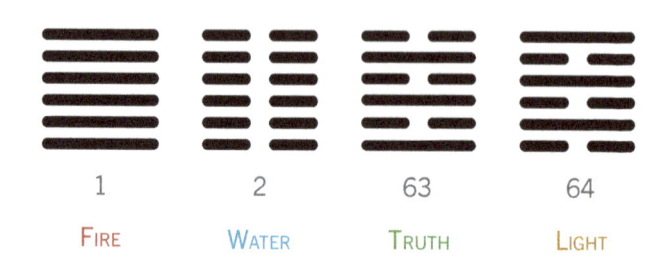

1	2	63	64
F<small>IRE</small>	W<small>ATER</small>	T<small>RUTH</small>	L<small>IGHT</small>

Around these four principles, all else is wrapped. All the codes are arranged into these patterns and squares.

The entire universe is nothing but one big board game made up of these patterns. And here are we, looking into these patterns.

The I Ching brings out these patterns beautifully, and these Gene Keys call out the dares for us all. It's like a pack of cards. Choose one, pick a card, any card – that's what the wizard says. Or else, play with them all. They all lead to the same place – they lead to awakening.

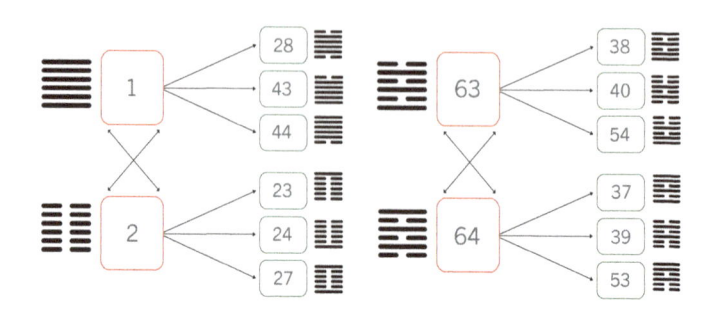

THE 4 PILLARS   THE 12 MYSTERIES   THE 48 LETTERS

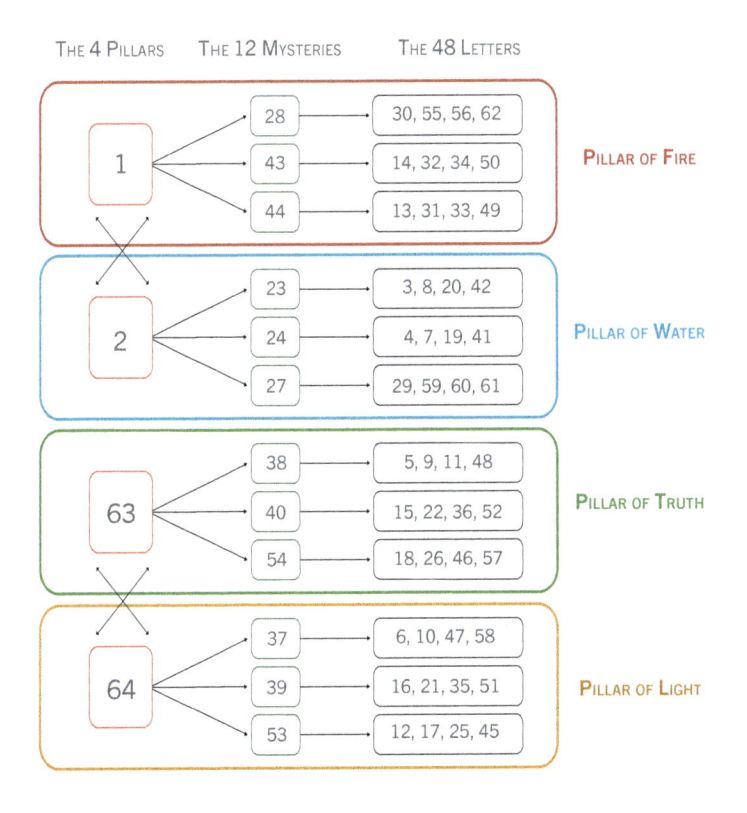

1	28 → 30, 55, 56, 62
	43 → 14, 32, 34, 50
	44 → 13, 31, 33, 49

PILLAR OF FIRE

2	23 → 3, 8, 20, 42
	24 → 4, 7, 19, 41
	27 → 29, 59, 60, 61

PILLAR OF WATER

63	38 → 5, 9, 11, 48
	40 → 15, 22, 36, 52
	54 → 18, 26, 46, 57

PILLAR OF TRUTH

64	37 → 6, 10, 47, 58
	39 → 16, 21, 35, 51
	53 → 12, 17, 25, 45

PILLAR OF LIGHT

THE NINTH DARE — DARE TO BE IMMORTAL

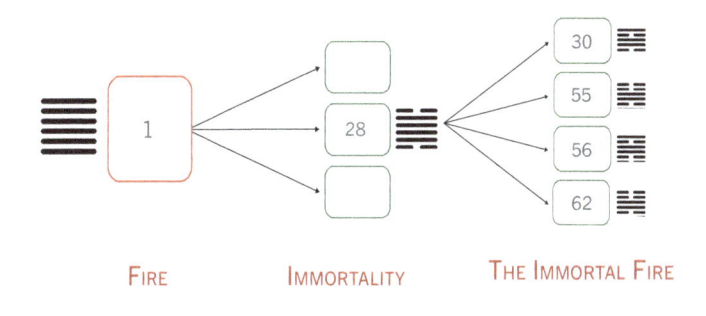

FIRE   IMMORTALITY   THE IMMORTAL FIRE

THE 30 — THE BLADE OF RAPTURE
THE 55 — THE BLADE OF FREEDOM
THE 56 — THE BLADE OF INTOXICATION
THE 62 — THE BLADE OF IMPECCABILITY

The Medicine of Purpose

Let's consider this 28th Gene Key and its Siddhi of Immortality that gives its name to this dare. It emerges from the field of fire, the Pillar of Fire. Remember, the 1st hexagram is hidden in the 28th hexagram, one of the twelve mystery Gene Keys in this formula.

What is the immortal fire? Consider yourself: you — the consciousness listening to or reading this. You are immortal. You cannot die. The return of the true human is the return of this truth concerning the illusion of death.

There is great darkness in this archetype — more fear perhaps than in any of the other gene keys. Our prime planetary fear is the ring-pass-not of death. Out of it comes our fear of the unknown and of demons, the working out of the horror genre, the idea of eternal damnation, of the dweller on the threshold, the vampire, the dark night of the soul, and all the traditional lower frequencies of immortality. It's our fear of the dark...

To escape the wheel of life and death, each of us must meet these demons. They are aspects of our karma. They are parts of us waiting to be integrated.

We also find in this gene key a prime health gate, residing deep in our immune system. This is our animal instinctive nature. It's an ancient survival-based fear. It has us believe that we have to struggle to survive, as we did in the past. This is where the 28th Shadow of Struggle comes from. Thus, fear is the root of all illness.

Yet when Homo sanctus comes there will be no illness and no aberrations. A new medicine of healing will begin to emerge on our planet – the medicine of higher purpose. And when you serve your higher purpose, you are serving love. You are being God. You are serving the whole. And as you serve, so your karma will be cleared – your wound will be unwound. All your aberrations will be eroded. It may take a few lifetimes but it is inevitable.

This ninth dare is wonderful. It contains four beautiful weapons to fight the darkness and cut ourselves free from the illusion of the maya.

I call these the Four Immortal Blades. You can use one or all of them to cut your attachments and sever your link to the fallen principle.

The Four Immortal Blades

30	The Blade of Rapture
55	The Blade of Freedom
56	The Blade of Intoxication
62	The Blade of Impeccability

If ever you feel the presence of dark forces, these blades are energies that you can call upon from within you. This is the God within you – the hero, the heroine, Homo sanctus, the blade wielder, the protector.

How to realise immortality?

THE 30TH SIDDHI – THE BLADE OF RAPTURE

The Blade of Rapture is rooted in the transcendence of our desire. In the I Ching this is the *Clinging Fire*. This is Fire over Fire in the Pillar of Fire.

Desire burns us over and over. Returning again and again into these forms, we are pulled by our desires – the desire for connection, for love, for sex and food, for power, for revenge, for freedom, and finally for truth. Rapture occurs when the fire is turned back upon itself. This is the old game of desires, and it never ends unless we ourselves end it.

And how we constantly hunger for change! Look at what new age types we are! Each time there's a full moon in this or that sign, or an eclipse or celestial event, we pour into it all our longing – 'this time will be the big change' – but it never comes. Major change won't come on the outside for a long, long time.

Remember, this is all relative. Your next incarnation may be in a thousand years. But on the inside, the change is here and now.

This is about allowing yourself to be burned, and to see the higher fire – the celestial fire – behind all desire. This requires the sustained practice of spiritual longing: the prayer, the fasting, the sacrifice, the supplication. The fire of our longing creates a discipline in us. It is not really enforced – the longing for inner purification just turns inwards. One day there comes a taste of it, of the rapture, and then we want more.

That rapturous discipline is a blade. Having felt it once, you can use the blade again. The more you allow it in, the more the blade cuts your illusion into ribbons.

Rapture builds inside us, from our higher dimensional bodies, from the buddhic and atmic planes. And thus the flame of our immortal nature is kindled once again.

Eckhart Tolle was born when the sun was in the 30th Gene Key. He was burned by the rapture. He reached the bottom of his desires and then the fires took him and this blade cut him free.

THE 55TH SIDDHI – THE BLADE OF FREEDOM

Doesn't the blade of freedom sound great? The sole purpose of the blade of freedom is to use it to cut ourselves free. This is already beginning to happen across the human genome. It is coming as a worldwide phenomenon. Freedom will change us all in time. Ultimately there is only one freedom: to know you are eternal. Nothing else will do. All else falls short. To be eternal is to be God. To be eternal is to be Love.

The dragonfly on the front of this book and all the gene keys books is an icon of freedom, as it symbolises our transcendence of the desire field – that's the water element that the dragonfly emerges from. The dragonfly takes to the air with our higher, unbounded nature, our illuminated consciousness.

This is the divine fire – the fire of the dragonfly adrift on the winds of God. This is our unchained awareness, cut away from our localised body – free to fly and merge with the whole, our true home.

What more is there to say?

I leave this one for you to contemplate...

THE 56TH SIDDHI – THE BLADE OF INTOXICATION

The 56th Siddhi of Intoxication works the other way from the 55. The 55 cuts away our attachments to the form, whereas the 56 moves deeper into those attachments.

This is about letting life cut you through moving deeper into life. This is about loving the form intensely. It's to taste pleasure and desire, loss and pain and even toxin so deeply that you transcend it just from going into it.

Life offers us so many distractions. This is about using those distractions consciously, rather than letting them pull us away from our centre.

When I was in my twenties I was a rather strange young man. I used to do experiments in awareness. I would go to airports, stations, and supermarkets and I'd meditate there. Sometimes I'd meditate sitting, sometimes standing, and sometimes doing. I particularly liked queues. I'd find the longest queue I could and stand in it and meditate with my eyes open. I'd be the only actor in the queue. It was a great experience because it made me realise that in life we are all actors. Moving through places where people are stressed or in a hurry, I played with this idea of immortality.

Sometimes I would do the game in a supermarket – I would walk around, fill up the trolley and in the end, I'd just put it all back. Once I was even a fake commuter. I got onto the train in my suit and took a ride into London, and then came back in the next rush hour. It felt deeply mischievous and mysterious. I had no work to go to, but I wore a suit and tie and carried a newspaper, all of it.

Since then, whenever I go into those places, I can tune in to that place of meditative awareness inside me. I am now a connoisseur of queues!

To be the consummate actor in the game of life – that's our deep purpose. To realise that you are immortal is to be the ultimate game player.

You learn to love all beings with such fire. No one escapes your fire, your love, even the most vehemently vitriolic person. All of it is fuel for the fire. It's all seen and understood as the dazzle of life.

As the awareness behind it all expands, so you learn to be an intoxicate – to get high on the lightest draught, to be drunk on the play of light on a leaf, or a drama unfolding, or even something uncomfortable. It all becomes fuel for your transformation. That is the wonder of the 56th Siddhi – divine intoxication.

Here's a fine example of this Siddhi – a Tibetan monk called Drukpa Kunley. Drukpa Kunley was an *intoxicant* – a man able to blend the mystic and the mundane in perfect symphony...

Drukpa Kunley (1455 - 1529)

Poem About Happiness

I am happy that I am a free Yogi.
So I grow more and more into my inner happiness.
I can have sex with many women,
because I help them to go the path of enlightenment.
Outwardly I'm a fool
and inwardly I live with a clear spiritual system.
Outwardly, I enjoy wine, women and song.
And inwardly I work for the benefit of all beings
Outwardly, I live for my pleasure
and inwardly I do everything in the right moment.
Outwardly I am a ragged beggar
and inwardly a blissful Buddha.

THE 62ND SIDDHI – THE BLADE OF IMPECCABILITY

This leads us to the fourth and final blade: Impeccability. This is to see the perfection of every tiny detail in life as an act of God.

All is part of God's grace fallen in the road before you. This is the perfection of the timing of every event in your life. This is the beauty of every feeling, of every illness, of every colour, every shape, every smell, every creature in its perfect element, and you moving through them all in perfect symmetry, including all your confusion, doubt, hate, pain, and fear – all of it!

This blade will cut away all your self-doubt, all your self-obsession, all your questing, and all your hunger until you become utterly accepting of everything.

This is the cold fire of clarity. This is the fire of moving closer and closer into the centre of the whole and watching behaviours and patterns that are rooted in ignorance dropping away, and knowing that they too are part of the perfect pattern. That's what impeccability is – it's to become more and more discerning. It's to pick up the discerning power of the great Masters, to move into your Impeccable being, and to claim your vulnerability as power. This is love down to the tiniest detail.

This 62nd Siddhi is also about all the many maps to the divine – Patanjali's yoga sutras or Richard Rudd's *The Gene Keys*. There are many exact maps, leading us inward – all transmissions of Impeccability. They contain tiny fires of truth that we can draw into every cell of our body, into every holon of our being, to bring about transformation.

Dare to be immortal. Dare to be homo sanctus. Do not wait for the future but use these blades now. Sever your very belief that you are separate at all, that you even need transformation.

The other thing about this Siddhi as I've contemplated it – is that it's all about languages. It gives us access to all languages – this is speaking in tongues. It can speak or understand any language because all languages are linked as fractals of one language – the language of light. Through this Siddhi also come ancient languages – lost languages – future languages, the languages of advanced life forms, and other galaxies. Here too are languages of geometry, of shape, of the hands and the body. All manner of languages hide here in this Siddhi. That's also something to contemplate.

The Ninth Dare

THE TENTH DARE – DARE TO CARE

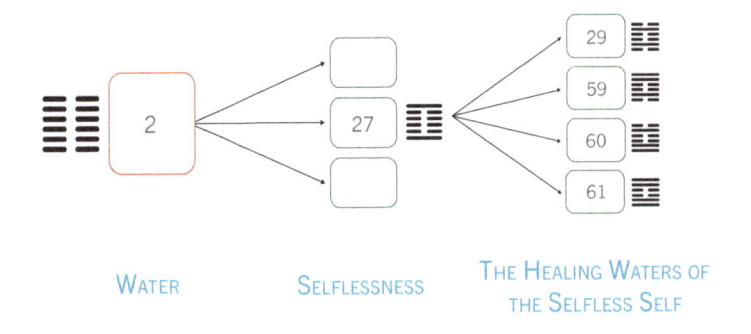

| WATER | SELFLESSNESS | THE HEALING WATERS OF THE SELFLESS SELF |

THE 29 – **DEVOTION** – BHAKTI YOGA

THE 59 – **TRANSPARENCY** – OPEN FOR BUSINESS

THE 60 – **JUSTICE** – JUDGEMENT DAY

THE 61 – **SANCTITY** – THE HOLY OF HOLIES

The Science of Service

And so, we move again from fire to water. In this element the language must change again, with the gene keys expressing the same truth from the feminine side, to balance out the fire.

The sixth race is already here. We call some of them things like the indigos. These are small flashes of brilliance, eccentric genius, and mutation that are appearing in these children who are coming through now. Gradually more and more will come.

Dare to care is going to change our whole society. We must learn to do things differently. We must learn, for instance, to care for the elderly by living with them not by pushing them away. We must learn to care for the young in a much better way. We talk a lot about caring for our children, but we don't. We push them into these tight boxes. We have to educate them and their parents in a completely different, free, and open way.

We also need an entirely new education around health care. We need a system of health care based on transcendence; a new Aquarian medicine that finds everyone a higher purpose and teaches us how to give birth and die consciously. This is how we will unpick our fear of death. And in time, we will learn all these things.

The new Aquarian medicine that's coming into the world is all based on water – on how to create the waters of life. Water is so powerful. Pure water can be magnetised to create incredibly potent essences. An example is the dew in the morning. There's nothing purer than the simple glistening essence that sits on the sunny, grassy meadows. It's an essence containing great healing purity.

To understand the new medicine is therefore to understand all these essences, and we must learn to drink the essences directly from nature. We can drink the frequencies that we need, the sounds that we need, the music we need, the colours that we need, and the food that we need. It's all about essence. We have to learn to bring balance to our system by taking in the right essence, to create harmony, to create a symphony inside our cells. This will be a whole new science of service.

This 27th Gene Key represents the movement from selfishness to selflessness, which is the primary role of homo sanctus. We will learn how to care for the mothers and the children, especially the incarnating child while it is still being programmed in the womb. Even today, more and more people are having conscious conception. The moment of conception is sacred. It's about focussing all your purest intent into the coming child. You prepare by doing *sadhana*, a spiritual practise, for weeks and months beforehand, and then at the point of conception, you can bring through this extraordinary, pure entity. Because you have created such a beautiful, clear vehicle, that little child grows into its highest possible manifestation.

As I was contemplating this 27th Siddhi, I came across this concept called the *annapurna siddhi*, which turns out to be a kind of mystical phenomenon. The annapurna siddhi is the Siddhi of Nourishment, which connects it to the 50th Gene Key whose name is also Nourishment (these two Gene Keys are powerfully connected in Human Design). Thus, both of these two Siddhi's have to do with this annapurna siddhi which is the providing of the abundance of food, or the mystical manifestation of abundant food. This Siddhi has been documented and recorded in many different places. The most common one we know is the five loaves and the two fishes that Christ manifested at the feeding of the five thousand.

NEEM KAROLI BABA

There have also been many other examples of this Siddhi. Neem Karoli Baba was someone who did this a lot. He endlessly produced sweets and chapatis and all kinds of things from under the blanket that he wore. He didn't just produce five or six, but all day long, all this stuff kept coming out from under his blanket! And it was always food. Another example is Swami Samarth, who has many similar stories involving him feeding his disciples from baskets that never ran out.

I mention all this because, despite the miraculous nature of this Siddhi, it's ultimately about service and caring. The food is a symbol of the abundance that lies within. It's a beautiful Siddhi to contemplate.

THE 29TH SIDDHI – DEVOTION
Bhakti Yoga

The first Siddhi to open here is the 29th Siddhi of Devotion. This means to care more deeply for God than for your small self.

Devotion only happens when your self-interest is completely out of the way. Commitment without the underlying love which impregnates it is not enough.

Can you dare to devote your life to the service of others? Bhakti yoga is the science and path of worship. Worship is a deeply misunderstood word and is often maligned by modern new-age mystics. Yet this path is open to all human beings and is probably one of the most accessible spiritual paths for people to identify with. You place your heart at the disposal of a visible or invisible higher being, and you make a continual connection to that being through your heart.

This is the path of the devotee, one who is willing and ready to receive the Master into the core of her heart and inner being.

The major religious paths are devotional – Hinduism, Christianity, Islam; although Buddhism (other than Tibetan) may be less obviously so. These paths are based on prayer, devotion, and love for the Divine.

The test of true devotion, however, is time. Can you walk your path through all the challenges, blocks, and tests that come your way? Can you stay beside that person through heaven and earth, through thick and thin? Can you keep your wedding vow in the Codon Ring of Union?

The Codon Rings are mysterious groupings of the Gene Keys. They are genetic families which link us collectively in different ways; for instance, this codon ring of union contains the 29, 59, 4, and 7. All four of these Gene Keys concern the new role of homo sanctus in relationships, and in all four, the lower trigram is water.

The 29th Siddhi is a *tantric* path – it is the path of surrender through our relationships. It takes huge courage to walk these paths because love will bring you again and again to your knees. These are wild paths, where few teachings exist and even fewer teachers. This is one of the new paths for the new human and for the new epoch. In a way, it's our new yoga. We *yoke* ourselves to these relationships and then we use them to transform us. We use the difficulty, the negativity, and the challenge to transform us, to purify us.

The Venus Sequence offers specific guidance along this path. Surrender to the beloved happens layer after layer as the heart softens and opens. Dare to care enables us to use our relationships as a means of letting go of old karmic negativity and moving into a rarefied frequency, what the Sufis call *fanah* – love as annihilation – the love which brings an end to the personal ego. Can we dare to care that much?

THE 59TH SIDDHI – TRANSPARENCY

Open for Business

Dare to be transparent. This 59th Siddhi is also in the Ring of Union. The new human, homo sanctus, will become transparent in so many ways. To come into union, we must drop all our secrets. No agenda can remain hidden inside us. Can you imagine that?

We have all heard stories about people coming before the Illumined Ones. The Master inhabits a world of transparency. He or she sees everything inside you. There is nothing you can hide: your shame, your hidden mistakes, and perversions, your negativity and fears... The Master knows it all. Can you imagine standing in that presence? Could you hold the gaze of such a being? When you can receive and return that gaze, you are becoming transparent. That presence is you. That transparency is how you need to be with yourself.

To be open and transparent, to have a clean heart is to drop all the secrets we generally try to hide. This 59 is the programming partner of the 55, where the Great Change is breaking through. Here in this pair of Gene Keys, a huge force of change will continue to ripple through human DNA for the next few centuries. Barriers will at first increase, then break down and dissolve in our communities, in our borders, in between our races and our ideologies. Union is coming.

In business, this trend is already powerful. It's not so easy to hide anymore. Tyrants can no longer hide their millions. Corruption is running out of places to hide. Power is falling away from the despots, from the selfish, from those who cling to it in desperation. Power is now moving towards the transparent, towards the humble, towards the empty.

Can you imagine our world in a hundred, a thousand years? It is going to look very different. We don't see it now. It seems that everything is in decline. But the opposite is true. Only the shadow is in decline. The higher consciousness catalysing this change is forcing us to search for meaning, for higher purpose. This union was always going to happen. It's making us dare.

Dare to be that open.

Dare to merge with all beings.

Dare to die into the collective.

Dare to be transparent.

Dare to care.

THE 60TH SIDDHI – JUSTICE
Judgement Day

Now we come to justice and judgement day. I love the flow of these stories.

Here is one of the great miracle Siddhis: the most unusually powerful one of all. This and the next Siddhi are in the Codon Ring of Gaia, so they involve big shifts in planetary consciousness.

The 60th Siddhi is hard for us to comprehend. The 60th hexagram is rooted in the prime yin force – water (*the Lake*). The trigrams are *Water over Lake*: the nuclear hexagram is 27, Selflessness, whose nuclear hexagram, in turn, is 2 – Unity.

Unity gives rise to selfless justice. Justice is a divine law underpinning every aspect of the cosmos, but this law is mostly invisible to human beings living within time. Because of the wheel of time, we do not always see the results of our actions or our karma over a single lifetime. The fruits of our actions often come later.

But time itself will begin to break down. As we become more transparent, the Siddhis bring us into the eternal now. In this timeless realm, we see and understand everything as just. Everything!...and then the beauty of this realisation floods us. It is a profound relief to know that everything is balanced by cosmic justice, the divine scales. Of course, life is fair. How could it not be?

Justice is selfless. Justice is compassion. We pay for everything we have done. By paying (which means suffering) we learn and grow – that is why we are here. Slowly we evolve into lucidity and selflessness. As greater numbers of us begin to do so, the 60th Siddhi is activated. This Siddhi is collective – it needs many of us to tip the scales. And then as we pass the tipping point, time and space begin to dissolve.

We are the ones who will crack the maya open: 'And I saw a new heaven and a new earth', as it says in the Book of Revelation. Earth changes will come, big changes, and the end of death as we see it – so many things will be torn open as we find our immortal body.

In my book *The Gene Keys*, I mentioned *Babaji* in this Siddhi. Babaji represents the immortal body that can move in and out of time and space.

THE 61ST SIDDHI – SANCTITY
The Holy of Holies

The Holy of Holies. This is the *shekinah* – the divine dove descending through the narrow gate. This is the camel coming through the eye of the needle. Only selflessness can take you through the eye. Occult knowledge is not enough. Pure love can bring you through. This is what sanctity is – homo sanctus. The earth will be purified because suffering purifies us all. Death purifies us all. Sanctity means to become whole, and when we are whole, we realise that we are without flaws. Then the higher bodies come down into your earthly vessel. Out of this purification, the new human will emerge – the sixth or trivian race – the sacred race.

Our holy ones throughout history are reminders of what is coming – of our future, of the true nature of humanity as eternal and all-loving, as just and caring. Dare to care. There is always a feeling of sanctity that surrounds holy people. The higher dimensions in the air around them are tangible, even after their death. Even the places where they lived retain their fragrance.

If you have ever experienced or felt this holiness, you will know what I mean. This 61st Siddhi carries its essence.

The Tenth Dare

THE ELEVENTH DARE – DARE TO BE A WARRIOR

A reminder of the four pillars once again as we now move to the Pillar of Truth – the 63.

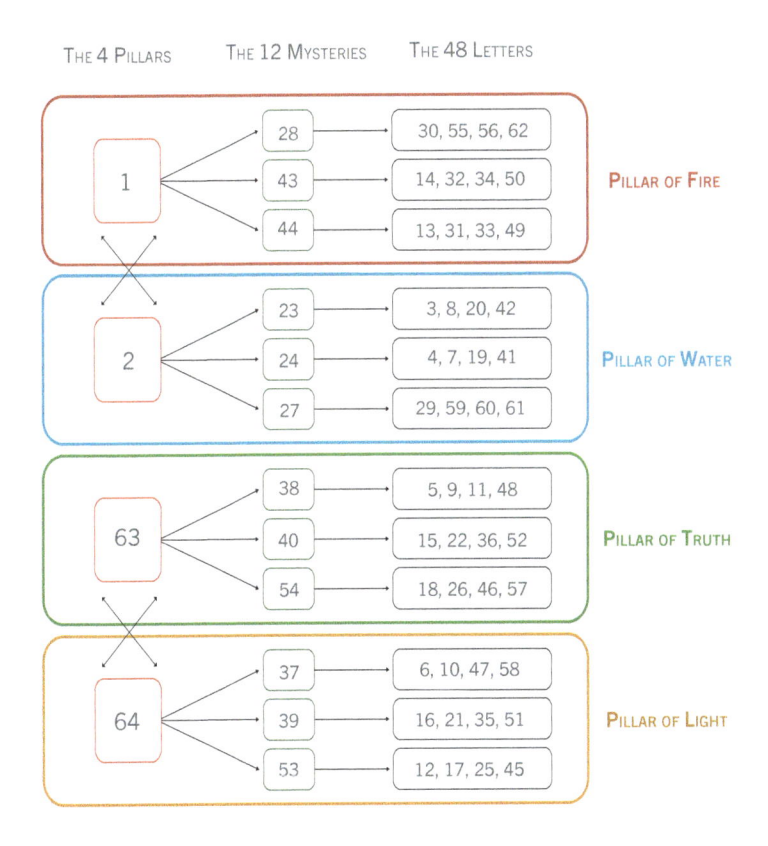

The 4 Pillars	The 12 Mysteries	The 48 Letters	
1	28	30, 55, 56, 62	Pillar of Fire
	43	14, 32, 34, 50	
	44	13, 31, 33, 49	
2	23	3, 8, 20, 42	Pillar of Water
	24	4, 7, 19, 41	
	27	29, 59, 60, 61	
63	38	5, 9, 11, 48	Pillar of Truth
	40	15, 22, 36, 52	
	54	18, 26, 46, 57	
64	37	6, 10, 47, 58	Pillar of Light
	39	16, 21, 35, 51	
	53	12, 17, 25, 45	

In this pillar are hidden another fifteen keys, with the 38 in the middle. Therefore, these next keys are rooted in the archetype of the spiritual warrior, brandishing the sword of truth.

I'm going to give you some warrior homework to do now. It's time for a tempo change. We've heard about all these Siddhis. We've been soaking them in. This next part is about action. You are challenged and invited to act on these frequencies.

TRUTH   HONOUR   THE HONOURING OF TRUTH

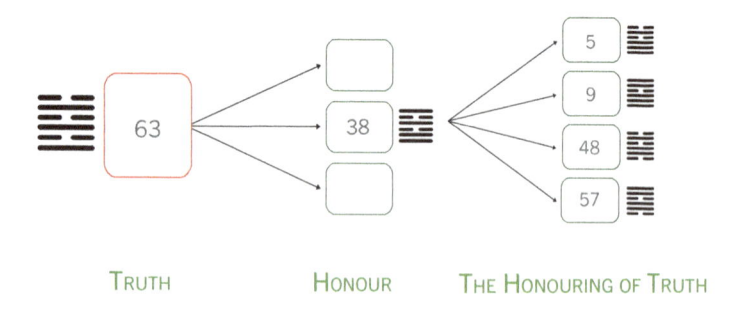

 THE 5 – **TIMELESSNESS** – BREAKING BAD HABITS
 THE 9 – **INVINCIBILITY** – LOVE IS IN THE DETAIL
 THE 48 – **WISDOM** – ACTING FROM NO MIND
 THE 57 – **CLARITY** – KNOWING THE FUTURE

THE 5TH SIDDHI – TIMELESSNESS
Breaking Bad Habits

We begin with the 5th Siddhi – Timelessness. This may sound like a dreamy permission to do nothing, just drifting in the divine currents but it isn't. It is about the way time is used from within timelessness. Clearly, you are born in a specific evolutionary time frame – and life presents you with opportunities within that time frame. You know there will be other lives. You can accept that eventually all humanity will transcend death and arrive at perfect union. You know that the universe will one day end and then begin again at another level, as all life does. These patterns and rhythms of truth are found within the 5th Gene Key.

Knowing all this, what will you do? Why not dance within time? Why not be a torchbearer for these truths? In your depth of patience, you know nothing matters – yet everything still matters. This is a great paradox. So you go out there and break or change a negative pattern. The 5th Gene Key awakens our awareness of patterns.

After watching this, after hearing this, go into your life as a warrior of light and raise the frequency of some mundane aspect of your life. Go on, I dare you!

Dare to be the warrior. Breakthrough into the timeless. This requires that we snap our addictive habits, that we break our attachments. That's the true power of this Siddhi. It blows your reality. It makes a mockery of the future. It laughs in the face of the past.

Do something now! Give up your negative, victim thinking.

THE 9TH SIDDHI – INVINCIBILITY
Love is in the Detail

The 9th Siddhi is Invincibility. The spiritual warrior's invincible goal is in fact to become utterly harmless. The spiritual warrior becomes a vessel for the loving act. Ra Uru Hu, the teacher of Human Design, used to say, 'Love is in the detail'.

In India, they call this *ahimsa* – the quality of care for small things – the utter respect for all living creatures – even for the smallest ant.

In his Yoga Sutras, Patanjali says: 'In the presence of a man perfected in ahimsa, enmity in any creature does not rise.'

Hence we hear the many stories of saints and masters lying down with wild animals and snakes. Indian folklore is packed with stories about snakes, especially cobras. The cobra hypnotises an ordinary person but becomes mesmerised by the ahimsa of the Master, and together they dance. There are many stories of the cobra coming into the Master's hut. Yogananda tells a number of them, and so do other good writers who wrote about their teachers.

Yogananda mentioned the mosquitoes. The mosquitoes never touched his master Sri Yukteswar. And when they were meditating and the mosquitoes would come in at night, they would be biting him, but they wouldn't go around his master. They never landed on his master's body. He noted this while he was being bitten all over! It was because of the power of his master's ahimsa. So, go out into your life carrying with you the power of ahimsa.

Sri Yukteswar

The next time someone comes at you with negativity, instead of flinching away defensively, lean into it and disarm them. Show them your invincibility. The more we emanate this perfection the more it impregnates our environment, the more we emanate our caring. Focus on the small things. The I Ching calls this 9th hexagram the *Taming Power of the Small*. Open a door for someone. Don't let that irritated word escape from your mouth. Spend a couple of minutes extra with that rather needy character. These tiny acts of kindness ripple out their blessings into our environment. The warrior has no need of defence. He or she is invincible by means of their great love.

Dare to be a warrior for love.

THE 48TH SIDDHI – WISDOM
Acting from No Mind

In the I Ching the 48th hexagram is called *The Well*. Wisdom emerges from the well. The warrior has so many names for this – the empty mind, harnessing empty chi, *shunyata* (the void), the Chinese Wu Chi...

In this Gene Key, the great mystery of *unknowing* comes into the form. This Siddhi and the 57 that follows it, are from the same codon group – the Ring of Matter. They both concern the bending of the laws of matter.

The 48 brings the unknown into the known – in that sense it is a pure empty channel. But it doesn't just channel knowledge. This is living wisdom. The whole being is moved by wisdom, by the 'empty force'. This 48th Siddhi can literally manifest something from nothing. Wisdom is a doorway. These people are also doorways to the other side. They allow you to see through the door into the void, into the mystery. They can even allow you to pass through the black hole across to the other side.

Wisdom has always been transmitted in this way – face to face, heart to heart, no-mind to no-mind. Wisdom is a transmission. One can't understand wisdom with the mind. It's beyond the mind, so one has to enter into its living transmission, and then it speaks from inside us. Homo sanctus, the future human, will live at home in this field, with the ability to know and see all things.

The 48th Siddhi can give you the pearl – the Pearls of Wisdom. Work with this gene key, work with this gift – the Gift of Resourcefulness. The next time you face a problem, sink into your well, into your wisdom. Sink into your void and see if a new way of tackling that issue emerges. Surprise yourself. You can't see what's down there in that well, but if you wait and you trust, it will emerge and then magic will appear on the Earth.

THE 57TH SIDDHI – CLARITY
Knowing the Future

As the 57th Siddhi of Clarity dawns, there is an absolute ending of fear. Where there is no fear, there is only clarity. Of course, this is the great goal of the spiritual warrior – to be fearless, to overcome fear. And fear lives within matter, within the form, within the body, within our memories, within the waters. Thus to purge fear is to break the bond with the body and overcome death.

The 57th Gene Key is a musical gene key. It's about attunement to frequencies – it's a tuning fork inside us. Whatever you tune it to, the body vibrates with that spectrum. So, to see through matter, to make the body transparent and empty is to see past the localisation of awareness. You tune it to the very highest frequency there is – to the Godhead. We are then invisible for we feel, sense, and become all things; and clarity is all there is.

The 57th Siddhi knows the future, not by reading it – by *knowing* it. How might it feel, to know your own and everyone's destiny? You might think that life would be a bit dull and boring, with nothing to anticipate, no story to unfold but that is from a dualistic viewpoint. The fact is there is no future. All form and drama are seen as illusory, like a dream.

The material realm is held together by *manas*, the cosmic mind-stuff. At high levels of frequency, thought is all-powerful. You think it, and it becomes. In this 57th Gene Key lies the secret of the philosopher's stone – the ability to manipulate all creation by reaching into the heart of the form principle and finding its emptiness. The philosopher's stone is no material thing. The stone is the realisation that all form is emptiness. The stone is this realisation!

Dare to be a warrior – fearless, deathless, eternal...
This is where humanity is heading.

When I was young, one of my favourite films was *The Magnificent Seven* – it's a Western based on the older classic Japanese film, *The Seven Samurai*. The original film was about noble warriors arriving to protect a village somewhere in China. The villagers hired a samurai. They hadn't much money because bandits were besieging them, so they hired just one warrior, and he had to use what he earned to hire six others. He chose them through a series of tests. In one of these, he and two or three of the samurai hid inside a house, having arranged to meet the new samurai there.

As he stepped into the doorway, they attacked him with their swords. If he could defend himself successfully, they would know he was the right one. At one point, a samurai came to the door and paused. Then he slowly turned around and walked off. He never went through the door because he had the 57th Siddhi at work inside him. The clarity sensed that that was not a door to step through.

We're like that. I loved that moment as a boy because I thought that the ultimate skill was to defend oneself but actually, the ultimate skill is to avoid the situation in the first place! As it happened, this man became one of the samurai. Anyway, these stories are fun.

THE TWELFTH DARE — DARE TO BREAK FREE

Finally, we reach again the Pillar of Light; the 64, Illumination leading to the 39 – the way of liberation through light.

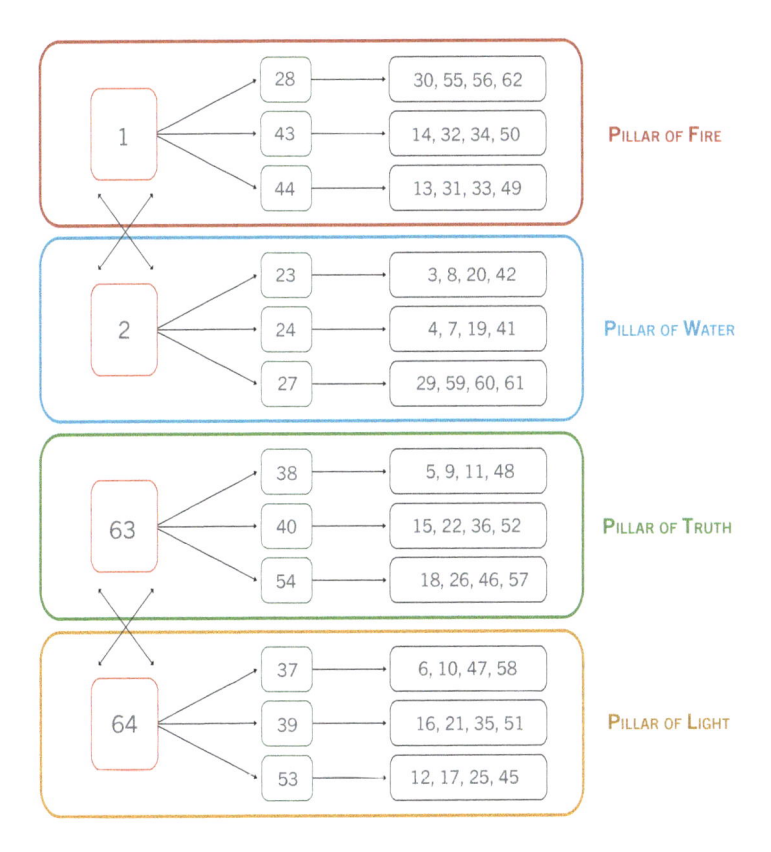

1	28 → 30, 55, 56, 62		Pillar of Fire
	43 → 14, 32, 34, 50		
	44 → 13, 31, 33, 49		
2	23 → 3, 8, 20, 42		Pillar of Water
	24 → 4, 7, 19, 41		
	27 → 29, 59, 60, 61		
63	38 → 5, 9, 11, 48		Pillar of Truth
	40 → 15, 22, 36, 52		
	54 → 18, 26, 46, 57		
64	37 → 6, 10, 47, 58		Pillar of Light
	39 → 16, 21, 35, 51		
	53 → 12, 17, 25, 45		

LIGHT   LIBERATION   THE LIGHT OF LIBERATION

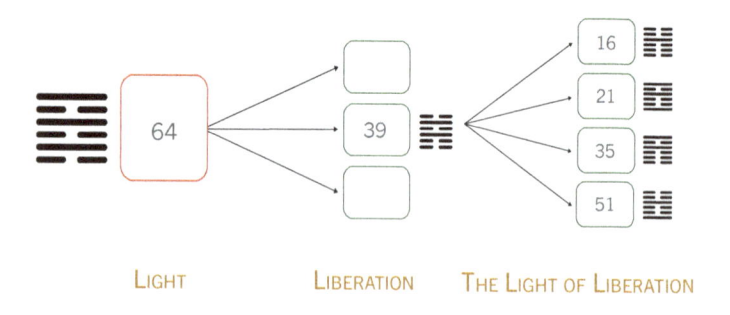

THE **16** – **MASTERY** – IF NOT NOW, WHEN?

THE **21** – **VALOUR** – IF NOT YOU, WHO?

THE **35** – **BOUNDLESSNESS** – CATCHING THE MIRACULOUS WIND

THE **51** – **AWAKENING** – LEAPING THE MOAT

Dare to break free. Dare to liberate yourself. This is the eternal dare. Every human being is dared this dare. Sooner or later we have to heed the call. There is a lot to liberate ourselves from – beginning with our concepts, ideas, and beliefs. Again, this is a proactive dare. Dare to liberate yourself, to cut away your belief structures, especially your spiritual ones. If you're a Gene Keys person, cut away your attachments to these teachings, cut away your profile. What if your birth time is all wrong? What if I sent you the wrong one just out of mischief?

If you are working with Human Design and you're told you are a projector so you have an idea you should sit there waiting for an invitation, or if you are supposed to behave and make decisions in a certain way – just let it go.

What if you got the wrong picture and it is someone else's? All your life you might be making that mistake, but when you are free there is no mistake. Drop your attachments to the form. Make use of them, enjoy them, but don't let them become a fixed worldview.

There are ways to get you to the edge – but then you have to let go. It is the same with gene keys. And if you are a vegetarian or a woman or a man or gay – see through the agendas that come with that form of vehicle, see through your concepts and realise these beliefs are all part of the window-dressing. You're not the dressing, you are beyond the dressing. So let your agendas fall away.

The new human will not be so easily led. He or she may play with wisdom but won't get stuck in it. We will take what we need and leave the rest. We will receive and recognise the transmission. It's never just the knowledge.

THE 16TH SIDDHI – MASTERY
If Not Now, When?

The 16th Siddhi is about not making excuses. The 16th shadow is easily distracted into indifference, sloth, and spiritual laziness. Sooner or later you will have to stop being a spectator and do the sadhana yourself. You are going to have to get up early and do your spiritual practice quietly inside yourself, over and over until you've made some inner progress. Nowadays we are all spiritual show-offs. I'm the ultimate one – so I'm going to burn for this – 'I've been to India, I did a retreat, I do Yoga, I'm a healer, I've got a teacher, I've found the ultimate technique, you've got to learn it.'

These are the kinds of things we say. I include myself in this! We need to shut up and stop all the nonsense. We behave as though spirituality is a lifestyle thing. Do you think Milarepa, the Tibetan sage, gave a damn about anyone as he sat naked singing his prayers and songs while the snow fell on his ice-cold, shivering, starving body?

We have to break out and find our own path, and then we quietly follow that path. Perhaps no one will ever know we are doing it.

Many are the secret yogis in the world who humbly follow their spiritual paths without any outward show.

One day we will have to let go of the techniques and move into the deep mystery where no paths are carved. Let the light awaken as you call out to it over and over again, until that force, or whatever it is up there, is so bored of listening to all your praying! Ok, let's give them what they want. Give it, for God's sake.

The Light of God is a call and response process. What do you think it takes to become a Master? This is the Siddhi of Mastery. The Master has to become an artist. The Master must learn to go beyond technique – their every breath must become a prayer of longing. Each gesture is imbued with their meditation. Their whole life becomes a constant contemplation on the centre, on God.

Dare to cut yourself free, and start now. Why wait? This Siddhi can draw from the 16th Gift of Versatility to borrow any other Siddhi, to be any of the 64; if you want the 13th Siddhi, the 12th, or the 8th... Mastery means that if you have mastered one, you have mastered them all – you can fly, you can do whatever you want. Did you ever dream of being an instant concert pianist? Any skill can be mastered through this Siddhi.

THE 21ST SIDDHI – VALOUR
If Not You, Who?

Now we come to the 21st Siddhi, Valour. We're victims of being led, and this is the dare to break free – to find the inner valour to break free and carve your own path across the wilderness. Be a rebel. Belong, but also be a rebel. That's what the Gene Keys community is all about. Belong, but be a rebel. Don't choose just one side, but be both. Can you follow me? No, you can't follow me. There is no way you can follow me. I have no idea what I'm doing, or where I'm going.

All I know is what I'm saying now, where I am right now – today. I'm just surfing the transmission. You have to let it into you, we each have to. Let it pulse in your bloodstream, let it open you, let it smooth you, let it have its way with you because we live in a world of sleepers. Step inside the inner circle and be a conduit. Stand tall and let the light shine through you, that's what you've got to do. Don't always stick to the things that are comfortable – your new-age friends, your new-age circles. We have to draw strengths from our circle, yes, but also we have to move beyond. We have to move out of our comfort zones into the *bog world*. We have to move into the world where people are suffering and sleeping, where they don't know about all this stuff.

So be the leader that the Divine wants you to be. Let the light speak through your words. There's a chicken outside my window right now going crazy... it's saying: don't be a chicken!

Let the Divine lay its hand on you and then you lay your hand on another in deep compassion. Be bold. Valour is about being bold. Be an early awakener, don't be distracted by your outer mission. Love it, let go of any fear or shame and wear your heart on your sleeve. Valour is love and courage together.

We're each knights and ladies of the Round Table and we carry our unique virtues out into the sleeping world, and there we have our adventures. We face our demons, our adversaries, and our challenges but then we also come back together around the Round Table, where we can share our stories, break bread and laugh together at the great drama that we find ourselves in.

We have to break free in order to have all of that. This is about not just being an island but also becoming a part of synarchy.

THE 35TH SIDDHI – BOUNDLESSNESS
Catching the Miraculous Wind

When we come to the 35th Siddhi everything just goes out of the window. If only we knew what we are capable of! We saw the 16th Gene Key that can break all laws and assume any Siddhi it likes. This is the ultimate miracle Siddhi – the Siddhi of Flight and Boundlessness.

Padmasambhava was said to have flown from Tibet to South America. Yogis and great sages have been witnessed flying through the air in their physical bodies. Many of us have had dreams where our bodies lift off into the air. These dreams feel so authentic because they are future memories. Because one day, in a future phase of our evolution, we will all fly through the air in our physical bodies. We will also move beyond even this one day. We don't need to fly, but this will be a breakthrough period. It's a miracle we have to move through, so for now it's enough to know that we can do it. (For health and safety, please don't go jumping off any buildings or roofs, I can't be responsible for that.)

The point is that this flight has to come from within the light itself. It's where the word comes from; flight-light. We have to become light and then we can float, and our thoughts will lift us.

The 35 can do more than this. This is the show-off Siddhi. If you can imagine it, then the 35 can do it. It is a wormhole whose only purpose is to show us the boundless. Miracles become visible under the laws of karma. You have to have earned a miracle, to be in the presence of the miraculous. And they come through like thunder. The one in whom the miracle is coming feels it long before it arrives. It rolls around in the valleys and slowly, slowly builds up, and then with a drumroll inside, the miracle comes thundering into the form.

This 35th Gene Key is a relic from an earlier evolution. It sits there in our DNA like the appendix in our gut. It's from an earlier epoch, where it was once our start codon. In other words, the 35th Siddhi dictated everything. Those magical Chinese films where the characters fly across the rooftops, that was us. We lived in a more merged time, long, long ago before the Great Flood. Our DNA was different then as well. Now we've become more complex as we have diversified and progressed. This gene key assured that. It has driven us with its hunger for progress. And our deepest hunger is to fly once again, to sail up into the sky and become one with the Divine, to be a bird in the skies of existence.

In the I Ching the 35th hexagram is called *Easy Progress* and it represents the sun rising over the Earth (Fire trigram over Earth trigram). One day as Homo sanctus, we will fly again. So for now, we can secretly smile to ourselves, and flow with the river as it is today.

THE 51ST SIDDHI – AWAKENING
Leaping the Moat

And finally, the 51st Siddhi. A beautiful one to end on. There is a beautiful, enlightened woman from Norway, Vigdis Garbarek and I happen to know that she was born with the sun in the 51st Gene Key, and a Norwegian friend of mine read to her about this Siddhi from my book. She said: I have no idea how the man who wrote that knows these things, but it is exactly the experience I have had in my awakening.

The 51st Siddhi deletes your illusions. I call this 'leaping the moat' because, in the Grail legend, the hero must leap the moat of the chapel perilous. The Grail is hidden inside the castle or the chapel. But the moat is filled with our fears, pains, and delusions like a river infested with crocodiles and snakes.

To dare to break free is to make these leaps of initiation across the void. Life will deliver us to the edge over and over again, but only we can jump. And in one sense, even we can't make the jump ourselves. The jump just happens. You have to jump over all your teachers. One day you just jump totally into God, into the light, into *fanaa*, into annihilation.

'Put on your jumping shoes and leap into the arms of God.'

Meister Eckhart

This entire teaching is ridiculous. The gene keys are ridiculous. They are wonderful, but they are what Goethe called 'the deeds and sufferings of light'. They are nothing but the words in a book about God. They aren't the real thing itself. They take us to the edge, but then... the jump must come on its own.

When I was in my twenties, I did a lot of breaking free. I would go with a small group of my friends to a cottage in the Scottish Highlands, like in the film *Braveheart*. We wore kilts and ran barefoot through the bogs and up into the hills and moors. We went often in the winter like this, like wild men and wild women. We used to jump into the waterfalls. We took these difficult initiations particularly in the winter when there was ice on the ground. It was deathly cold up there in the Highlands in December. We found a special place – a double waterfall that dropped into a small pool. It was a five-metre jump down into the pool, and sometimes we would go there at night. It was dark, windy, and ice cold. You wouldn't even want to be out there in thick clothes. But we stripped naked and dared each other to jump into that darkness, into that annihilation.

You never forgot your first jump because the fear was so intense, it gripped your whole body. You are perched on the void, freezing, saying to yourself; if I jump in there, I'm going to freeze, I'm going to die, I might die. Luckily, no one did!

Anyway, you jump, or the jump happens. But you might be standing there for twenty or thirty minutes, it was different for everyone. You'd stand there shivering, then you'd see one person jump and you would hear their cry of elation and you could hear them below, but you couldn't even see them getting out – all you could hear was them shouting and whooping with release. You either knew you would do it, or you didn't. Many people didn't: they took their clothes off and put them back on again, or some didn't take their clothes off, but they came along. They were equally embraced by all of us because just to be there with your fear was enough. You didn't have to do it, it was dangerous, it was crazy, you could die or have a heart attack, it was so cold. Being at the edge of the fear, and the jump, the jump was something that just occurred. That had extraordinary power. I felt it the first time I had to stand there, standing in the fear until the jump happened.

That is the 51st Siddhi. Standing there inside the fear, you confront it until the fear has finished with you. Then the jump is there, and you break free. You cross the moat and you find the Grail inside. In Scotland, we found an immense heat. In that amount of cold, the inner heat exploded from inside our bodies into our bones. We felt invincible.

Dare to break free!

Part 4

The Final Four Dares

Earth Ascending

Dare To Be Divine

EARTH ASCENDING

Welcome to the final four dares.

The new human, Homo sanctus, is coming, and with it comes the notion of ascension.

Each of these final four dares is an element of the ascension process. But by now, we can perhaps understand that this is no longer only about us. All beings are caught up in this grand plan. The whole of Gaia will ascend, as all the hierarchies ratchet up another gear. Plants will become animals, animals will become humans and humans will become angels. All kingdoms are caught up in this great ideal of heaven coming to Earth. The chain of evolution that lies beyond each kingdom of nature suddenly becomes embodied as the higher power of involution spiritualises the form principle. Even the densest layers, such as those in the mineral realms, which were dormant, suddenly take on life.

None of this is how we can imagine it though. Minerals don't literally become plants. Rather the life force which was buried within them begins to glow. It's the essence that's the key. It's the same essence that shines through all forms but it's just refracted differently through each stratum of life. So the very rocks on which we sit will become radiant, and the whole of Gaia will become a great glittering pageant.

Once again, we contemplate the four pillars of the temple of existence: the two pairings formalised in the I Ching – fire and water, truth and light.

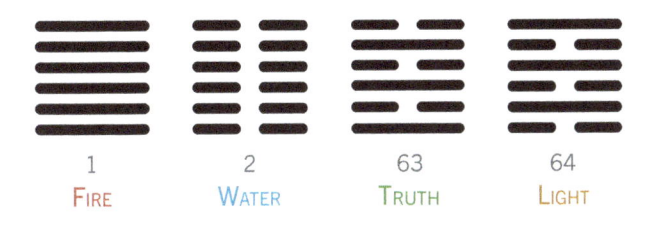

1	2	63	64
Fire	Water	Truth	Light

As I mentioned earlier, I call the Gene Keys collectively *The 64 Names of Love*. We should remember that no single name is favoured above any of the others. In the Gene Keys transmission, we use our profiles and the Golden Path to describe these evolutionary arcs, but when we come to the siddhis, we can throw all that away. Any of the 64 names will do.

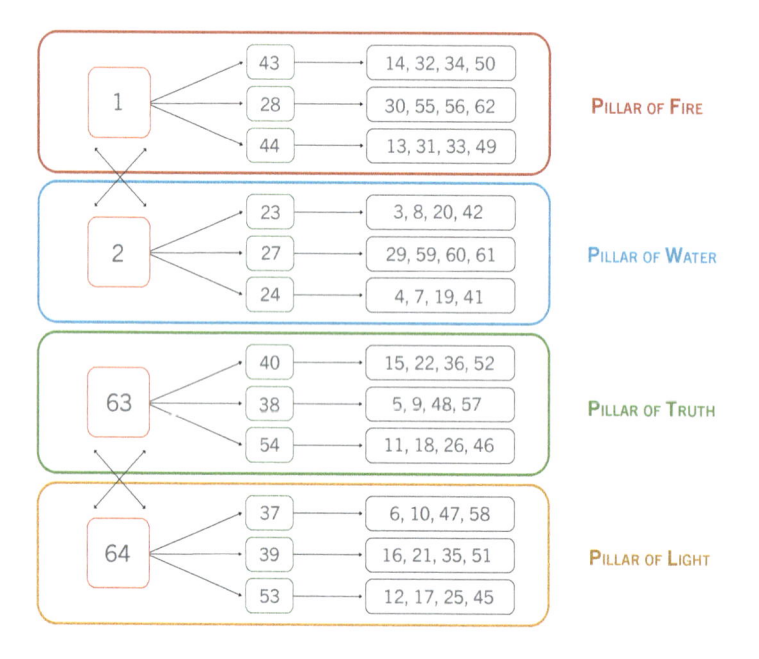

1	43 → 14, 32, 34, 50		
	28 → 30, 55, 56, 62		PILLAR OF FIRE
	44 → 13, 31, 33, 49		
2	23 → 3, 8, 20, 42		
	27 → 29, 59, 60, 61		PILLAR OF WATER
	24 → 4, 7, 19, 41		
63	40 → 15, 22, 36, 52		
	38 → 5, 9, 48, 57		PILLAR OF TRUTH
	54 → 11, 18, 26, 46		
64	37 → 6, 10, 47, 58		
	39 → 16, 21, 35, 51		PILLAR OF LIGHT
	53 → 12, 17, 25, 45		

If you do the Gene Keys Ambassador Programme, you will see that at the end, before you assume your seat at the Ambassador Circle, you are invited to pick three siddhis, and you agree to represent those Siddhis at the table within our synarchy.

Synarchy can only be built upon the rock of the Siddhis. You are charged to uphold that frequency, as in the stories of knights and ladies of old, where each knight or lady represented a different virtue.

The siddhi that you choose may or may not be in your Gene Keys profile. None of that matters at this level. Just one name of love is enough. One is the same as all.

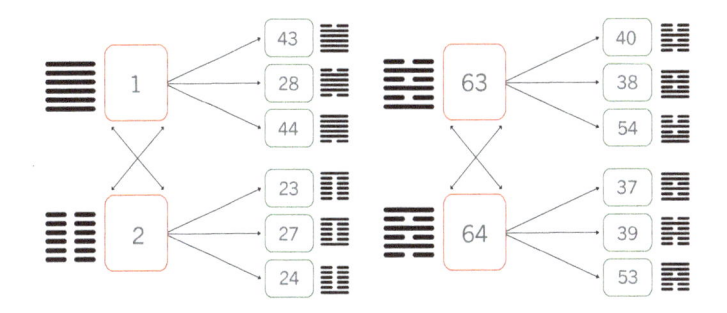

You can pick up the theme of this final chapter already by glancing at the four nuclear siddhis: the 44, Synarchy; the 24, Silence; the 54, Ascension; the 53, Superabundance. Synarchy brings silence. Ascension leads to the vision of superabundance. Use any other iteration you like of those four words.

THE THIRTEENTH DARE – DARE TO BE CHOSEN

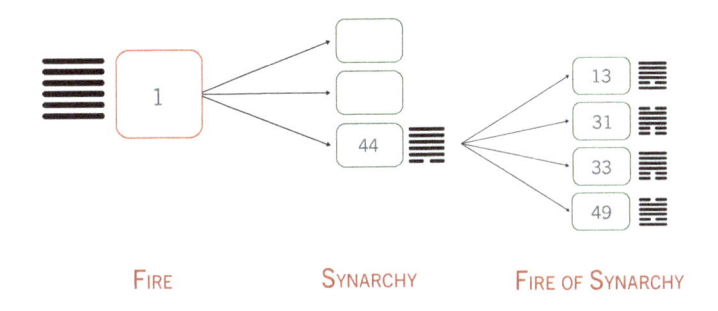

FIRE   SYNARCHY   FIRE OF SYNARCHY

THE 13 – **EMPATHY** – FRACTAL RELATIONSHIP

THE 31 – **HUMILITY** – THE ROUND TABLE

THE 33 – **REVELATION** – TOTAL RECALL

THE 49 – **REBIRTH** – THE NEW WORLD ORDER

Once again, we begin with the principle of fire. We see here that the underlying principle of synarchy is not water but fire. This is interesting to ponder. As all things have this secret fire at their core, synarchy is the perfect aligning of the principle of hierarchy. It brings together the two principles of hierarchy and heterarchy – the vertical principle and the horizontal principle.

It is rare for people to understand this. They tend to think that synarchy is a kind of heterarchy, where everything is fair and balanced, all people are equal and there is no leadership. But that is not how it works. For instance, neither communism nor capitalism by themselves is perfect, but a blending of the two could create a balanced society. The vision behind communism is fairness, equality, and balance. The vision behind capitalism is freedom. Synarchy combines these two visions – not their forms but the principles beneath them.

Synarchy burns us. It burns up the ego. Ascension requires us to leave behind our identification with any separate forms. There is the vehicle wrapped around you, and its placement within the overall story; but the indwelling awareness is the same in all forms – it's the age-old paradox of being both the ocean and the drop.

The point is that synarchy is fiery. I don't want you to think that synarchy is some cute state where everyone has their say and decisions are only made by consensus. Synarchy has a very clear inner structure but it's not imposed by the ego, by any ego. It comes about naturally as selfless leaders appear. Selflessness is a fire because its love burns the ego out.

And so, to the thirteenth dare – Dare to be chosen.

THE 13TH SIDDHI – EMPATHY
Fractal Relationships

The first of the principles underlying synarchy is empathy. Empathy is the first kind of fire. Empathy means that you are with another *inside* them. That's what the prefix *em* means as opposed to *sym*, from sympathy which means *with*.

The 13th Gene Key is *The Fellowship of Man* in the I Ching. It's the Council Fire of the Elders, and we will all sit round this fire, which is our selfless vision of service to the whole.

This is *arachne*, the thirteenth sign of the zodiac, the spider sitting in the heart of her web listening to everything and everyone. When she sees even a tiny spot of ego appear, she pounces. This is the fire of self-awareness. You can't be empathic without being deeply self-aware.

As a siddhi, the 13 builds synarchies. Its vast openness connects people, creatures, and all things together. Empathy, therefore, means that we learn to listen to the whole.

It is appropriate that our 13th dare starts with this siddhi because this dare is full of symmetry. When you dare to be chosen, you as the Master form your own fractal around yourself. The honey of your empathy draws all manner of bees to you. The bees choose you. This is how leaders in the synarchy rise. They do not thrust themselves forwards. They appear because people surround them and naturally trust in them.

This is all about relationships. You can't be empathic and not love relationships. No relationship is too much for you if you have the 13 in your profile. The karma of your relationships is pure gold, and you harvest it in order to become more empathic. And the more empathic you become, the vaster your love expands. Thus synarchy is built through fractals – through those karmic relationships which form circles of trust and beauty.

The hallmark of true synarchy is that others choose you. You never choose yourself. Life chooses you.

Dare to be chosen.

THE 31ST SIDDHI – HUMILITY
The Round Table

From 13 to 31 is another nice symmetry. In the 31st Gene Key, we ask, 'What is true leadership?' We need to have inspirational leaders. Synarchy requires hierarchy, a hierarchy of humility. The hub of a circle is the only part that never moves. The centre is essentially empty. In the same way that it is now believed that every galaxy has a supermassive black hole at its core.

This is the power of humility. You can't do a spiritual exercise and become humble. It simply happens. It is a selfless event – a non-event.

Those who are true leaders naturally rise to the top, or perhaps we should say, they rise to the centre.

Of course, it isn't like this now in our society. The opposite is the case. Political and national leaders force their way to the top, through cleverness or charisma. But the future leaders; all are and will be reluctant *messiahs*. They recognise that everyone is as important as everyone else. The smallest ant is part of the beauty of all beings, so every creature is treasured. This is humility, the emptiness. The vision at the Round Table is of equality inside but not on the outside. The mistake of communism, for example, is to say that as we are equal on the inside, we should force that onto the outside and all become the same.

Hierarchy brings colour, depth, and story; it also brings drama to the story. Hierarchy and heterarchy – one serves the other. This isn't a top-down hierarchy, it is a circular, spiral hierarchy. The one at the centre serves the next one out, and the one further out in the pattern serves the one further in. We serve each other equally, but we all play different outer roles. The greatest humility is in serving another. When someone serves you selflessly it creates vast gratitude in you, and this gratitude is the currency of the new Earth.

This is about the model of the gift economy. The gratitude generated by selfless service makes the synarchy super-efficient because everyone does everything for free. But it only works when everyone does it.

To be in synarchy is to be in bliss. It doesn't matter what your role is in the Divine hierarchy. Whether you are a leader or a follower, it doesn't matter. Whether you are a janitor or a king, bliss is bliss! The outer role is simply a cloak. We are all actors in the great game. Consider the way decisions are made among the council of angels. Do you think they disagree?

They simply tune into the collective direction coming through the totality. Everyone is the centre. This paradox is the truth. That is how the Earth will begin to ascend – when humanity begins to form these Round Tables, these fractal groupings of selfless service, these Divine synarchies.

THE 33RD SIDDHI – REVELATION
Total Recall

Now we come to the 33, another symmetry. We've had both the 13 and the 31 and now we come to the 33. This is Revelation. This is how the past reshapes the future because the past contains all the secrets, all the seeds. We must recall our past. Once we recall our past lives, we can see where we're going. We can see the synarchy. We can see the Divine plan.

When you can only see one life, you have no sense of perspective. You may even think that this life is all there is – just this one life. How stingy that version of the world seems! Here you are, you get one life, that's it. It's not very generous, is it? No wonder our world is so selfish today; because so many believe this to be the truth. However, once the memory of Revelation has awakened inside you, suddenly it's all very, very different.

You know what memory is like – it comes as a flood. These are karmic memories stored in our bodies, but the body has to become pure first for the memory to reawaken. This 33rd Siddhi is unusual, in that its nature is collective, so we *all* have to be purged.

On the next page, you can see the codon rings – these are mysterious karmic linkages between all the gene keys. They are grouped into families according to their genetic combinations, and all these families of gene keys have specific names.

The 22 Codon Rings

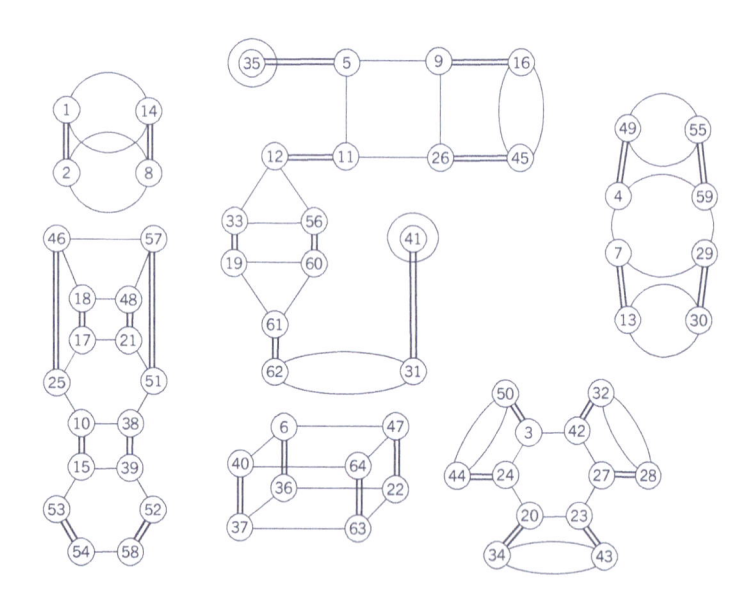

Here are the two codon rings known as the Ring of Trials and the Ring of Gaia: again, we see two 'threes' – another symmetry. But I want you to think about this. Why is the Ring of Trials linked to Gaia? It is because Gaia is predestined to pass through many trials.

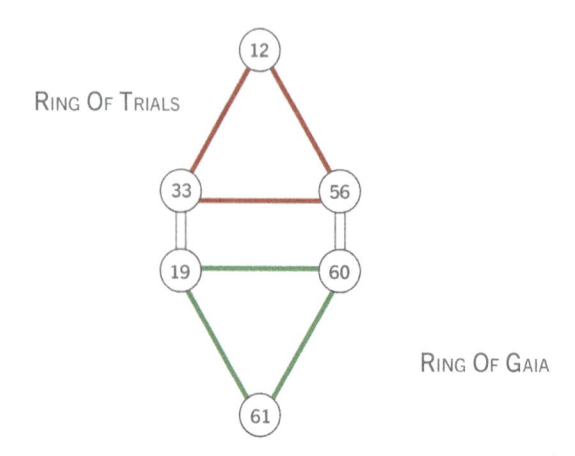

Ring Of Trials

Ring Of Gaia

This planet holds many memories. We have forgotten what we really are – where we came from. In our descent into matter, we have forgotten that we are gods. So, we will have to remember. This is the Siddhi of Revelation, and the 33 is a master number, as is the 44.

The synarchy has to be remembered. All the members of the synarchy have to recall who and what they are, and then assume their correct seats at the Round Table.

As soon as we start to form these groupings across all cultures, great revelations will come. We are meant to find each other – to come to meet in the flesh. *Coming to Meet* is the original name of this I Ching hexagram. The memories can only come through direct aura-to-aura contact. Our collective signatures are awakened only when we come together. This is why Gene Keys gatherings are so powerful because when we re-join our limbs for a few days, the Revelation comes. It doesn't come through the mind or any system of knowledge, but through the physical cellular contact – the memory.

Here we can also see how the 33 is directly linked to the 19 – Sacrifice. This points to big Earth changes. We have to remember once again that we do not die – that we are one being endlessly sacrificing itself to give birth to something higher. Welcome the beauty of the story!

Mooji, whom many of you will know, has a profile with a 19/33. This is why so many people go to him – for the memory, for the Siddhi of Revelation. It is not the teaching. It is always the presence, the memory. He's a lovely man.

Dare to be chosen.

THE 49TH SIDDHI – REBIRTH
The New World Order

The final part of this chapter heralds a rebirth – a new fractal coming into the world, a new Earth, a new set of numbers – a new code.

The 49th Siddhi is huge. Through its Codon Ring – the Ring of the Whirlwind – it's linked to the 55th Siddhi of Freedom. We are going to go through this whirlwind, both as individuals and as a species. There is no choice in this. We will remember ourselves, and we will rebuild the world in a higher image – in the image of God.

SRI AUROBINDO

Sri Aurobindo, another favourite man of mine, was born on the 49/4 axis and carried a great vision of the future human into the world.

AUROVILLE

Auroville is an experimental city based on a vision of humanity living in unity. It was inspired by Aurobindo. I've never been there but would love to visit. It is an early attempt at rebirth – of a new way of living – with all nations represented, and a fractal architecture that mimics a higher consciousness.

Quite a few of these experiments are already appearing in the world, like Damanhur in Italy, another example.

There is a great example of this 49th Siddhi in the life story of Desmond Doss, a pacifist who served in the US Army during World War II. There is now a film about his life called *Hacksaw Ridge*. Desmond refused to carry a rifle or do harm to another human being. He served as a medic in the Pacific Ocean theatre of World War II and survived horrendous conditions to save countless lives on the battlefield. Where other men retreated, he alone went back into enemy territory to save lives. He even saved the lives of the enemy. The aura of such sacrifice and selflessness creates a protective shield. Desmond survived the war to tell his tale and inspire many others by his selfless example.

The New World Order will emerge in the future: it is emerging now. This is the beginning time of the great mutation.

The new human will need a new Earth, a new medicine, a new education, a new social structure that is nothing like that which went before. There will be immense upheavals on our Earth. That which is coming has no similarity to that which is here now. The new economy will be based on love. There will be no money, nor any need for it. We will use the benefits of our technology to free ourselves to go inwards and recall our source.

We can see the early stages of this new order emerging around us, even as the old models crumble. The 49th Siddhi is giving rise to this rebirth. Rebirth means that what comes bears no resemblance to what came before. In the same way, when we awaken, that which we become is not like that which we were. Once you've remembered, forgetting is gone – forever. We still have to live, we have to do the same things, but the indwelling consciousness is completely different.

To Dare to be chosen is a paradox. We don't choose, so how can we dare?

We simply have to dare to be reborn.

THE FOURTEENTH DARE – DARE TO BE SILENT

The 4 Pillars of the Temple

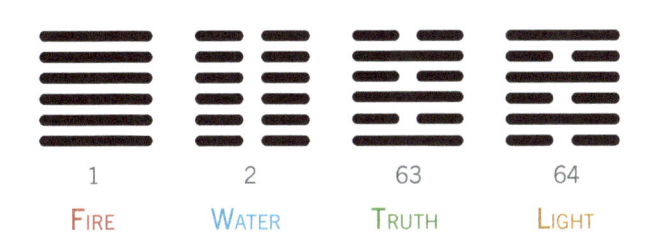

1	2	63	64
Fire	Water	Truth	Light

We now move once again from fire to water, to the 2nd Gene Key of Union and its daughter the 24, Silence.

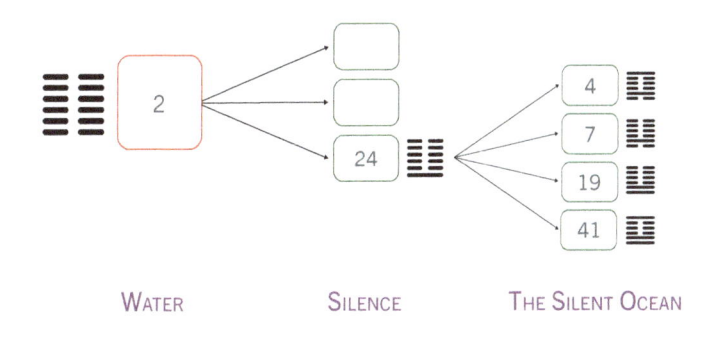

Water — Silence — The Silent Ocean

THE 4 – **FORGIVENESS** – RETURNING NON-LOVE WITH LOVE

THE 7 – **VIRTUE** – AN ARMY OF VIRTUES

THE 19 – **SACRIFICE** – THE SILENT TSUNAMI

THE 41 – **EMANATION** – THE GOLDEN GOOSE

Silence and water are linked, as are silence and union: the silent union of water and the silent oceanic embrace.

This is dare to be silent – our fourteenth dare. What is more silent than the feminine, than the void?

THE 4TH SIDDHI – FORGIVENESS
Returning Non-Love with Love

Thus we move from union to the Codon Ring of Union. This is a group of four gene keys that relate to the new relationships that are coming into the world. 'Earth Ascending' requires a rebirth in the way that we relate.

The 4th Siddhi of Forgiveness brings an end to all issues. You don't end with forgiveness – you begin with it. You don't wait for issues to arise and then do the forgiving. Forgiving is the basis, the ground of our relationships. Whatever happens, it is already forgiven. That is the nature of love. To live with such a being who embodies this level of forgiveness is to learn the meaning of silence. Forgiveness brings crystalline silence and simplicity to all human interactions.

The 24th Gene Key is about incarnation (the hexagram is called *Returning*). We return to the form over and over in order to be forgiven, in order to learn, to evolve, and to purify our essential nature.

We can't learn something as exquisite as forgiveness in just a single lifetime – it takes tens of thousands of returning lifetimes to polish the mirror of our inner awareness until we can remain in the deep silence. I don't know any quality that can benefit relationships more than forgiveness.

The 24th Shadow is the addictive mind, the mind that won't let go. But as soon as you see the higher pattern behind these shadows, you can break out of them.

The 24th Gene Key has a special line – line six – it's called 'The Pearl of Great Price'. This is the harvest of forgiveness. Suddenly neurosis is gone and only silence remains.

So our task is simply to go on inquiring towards God. Seek and ye shall find. Forgive yourself and all shall be forgiven.

Much illness is caused through non-forgiveness. When Jesus was asked: 'Shall I forgive him seven times?' he replied 'No. seventy times seven!' This is what we mean by the expression returning non-love with love – we turn the other cheek... We go on forgiving over and over.

THE 7TH SIDDHI – VIRTUE
An Army of Virtues

Next, we have Virtue, the 7th Siddhi. Behind all true leadership lies virtue.

Virtue is based on empathy (its programming partner is the 13th Gene Key). When you realise that virtues and vices are actually living beings, you begin to understand why this hexagram is called *The Army*. Your virtues are your army. They are inside you. They keep you healthy – they prevent the addictive mind from taking over.

The spiritual heart is the army, and Divine thought is the general. This is a gate the angels work through – it's the Gift of Guidance.

The Chinese say that the body has its own spirits – that each organ has its own inner virtue. The more you polish the virtues of these organs, the more radiant you become. This is why there are stories of the bodies of the saints never decaying – they are so pure that no bacteria can take hold.

This notion is found in the *vedas*, and in so many spiritual paths – the notion that goodness creates a purifying energy field around us. Good karma is generated through virtue, which generates merit, which over the course of many lives brings us closer to those who are holy and to those who are pure – to the Masters.

I find it amazing that even in spiritual circles these days, this way of thinking is overlooked. Goodness and benevolence have fallen out of vogue. The emphasis now is more on freedom. I'd like to bring benevolence back and put it in its rightful place at the heart of the spiritual path.

The power of virtue is incalculable. A virtuous act is a selfless act, and a selfless act stands the test of eternity. If you die selflessly, your next birth will be ripe and the conditions you create for yourself will be hugely beneficial.

Thus do our relationships offer us this great opportunity – to polish our virtues and to die over and over again into that which is higher.

THE 19TH SIDDHI – SACRIFICE
The Silent Tsunami

What is sacrifice?

It flows in the same vein as virtue. Any good deed is a sacrifice. You surrender your sense of selfishness in order to serve the whole.

The origin of all religious sacrifice is in fact sensitivity to animals. It's the root of all ancient shamanism – this pact we make with death. The spiritual power in true sacrifice is awesome because we have to die into our higher selves.

Every time you think life is giving you a hard time, try and change your attitude. Give yourself into the experience, heart, and soul. Be willing to die for something higher than you, and then you will experience the Divine coming down *into* you.

There is no way to the higher realms without some form of sacrifice. Sacrifice isn't a technique you can just 'do'. If you make a sacrifice and it's not from your heart, it has no power to transform you. You have to give something that is precious to you.

You cannot give up an addiction (the 24th Shadow) – you can only transfer it to a higher plane.

The mystery of sacrifice is that it is rarely visible. Someone attacks me and I send him pure thoughts in return. Who can see this? He cannot. But my intention is sacrificial. Thus sacrifice is usually unseen. You have to sacrifice what others think of you, but redemption always comes in the end.

I always think of the great lion Aslan in the novel by C.S.Lewis *The Lion, the Witch and the Wardrobe* – of how he willingly lays down his life to the evil Queen, and then of course he is reborn through that sacrifice.

Thus all true sacrifice generates a tsunami. It will return to you, and when it does, the power of its siddhi will cause nothing but awe, both inside you and inside others.

THE 41ST SIDDHI – EMANATION
The Golden Goose

The Siddhi of Emanation – this is the emergence from the chrysalis. You are an infinite source of butterflies! You are the golden goose. The eggs keep on coming – the eggs are our dreams, and if you are not attached to them, they will come true. Our dreams come directly from the Divine when they are not self-serving.

In any group or community, your dreams provide an initiating power filled with excitement and enthusiasm.

Your emanations hold the dreams of the collective. Each dream is made of light and if you are unattached to it, it remains pure. If you become over-attached to the outcome, you will end up wishing for the future, rather than being here now, and the dream cannot then manifest.

The 41st Gene Key is the Initiator Codon in DNA. It is unique in this way. In the tarot, it's represented by the figure of The Fool, who must follow his or her emanation back to the source – which is the essence of every spiritual teaching. This siddhi is about following one's emanation back to the source. This is what a Master is – an emanation of the source.

You can taste that silence in the Master. It's deafening. It's blissful. And we are drawn to that flame over and over again, life after life, until we reach back into the source and vanish into that silence.

True silence is not about the absence of sound or thought. The world is actually the sound of thought. Silence is the atmosphere you enter after you have reached escape velocity. The thoughts that impregnate silence are Divine thoughts– they are akin to love. 'No mind' is a concept deeply misunderstood. These then are the paths to silence:

The 4 – you forgive yourself and everyone else around you.

The 7 – you cultivate your virtue to overcome your vice.

The 19 – you sacrifice your own needs for the sake of others.

The 41 – you are ready to emerge from your chrysalis
(the dragonfly).

Dare to be silent. Dare to return to your source.

The Fourteenth Dare

THE FIFTEENTH DARE – DARE TO ASCEND

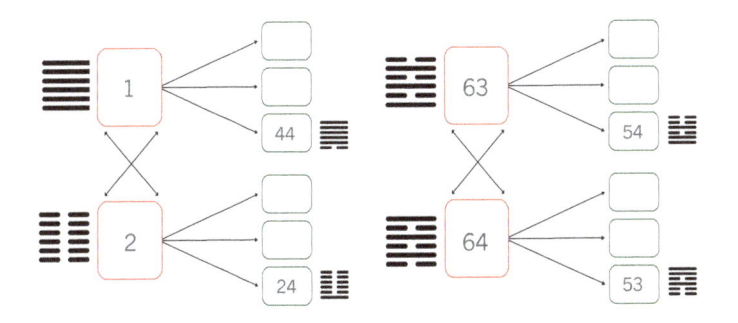

Here we return to the 63rd Gene Key – to Truth – and to Ascension, the 54. This is dare to ascend.

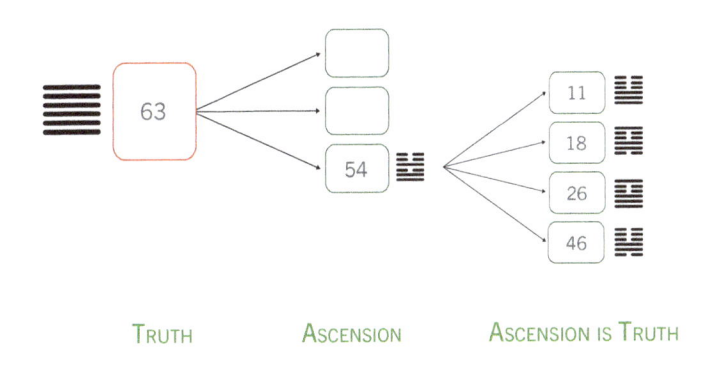

TRUTH   ASCENSION   ASCENSION IS TRUTH

THE **11** – **LIGHT** – WHITE MAGICK

THE **18** – **PERFECTION** – THE PERFECT PARADOX

THE **26** – **INVISIBILITY** – THE EARTH GRID

THE **46** – **ECSTASY** – EATING MANGOES

This is our penultimate dare. Truth is ascension… We have to ascend into the Truth.

I know I am asking a lot of you and myself in this course. But it's time to come out of the closet.

Some fifteen years ago, while I was out running, a powerful being whispered into my ear my name – followed by this incredible concept – *dare to be divine.*

The 54th Siddhi has a great Divine ambition – nothing short of the *transformation of matter* – to make the whole Earth shine again. It brings back these knights and ladies to the Round Table, and it brings with it this urge – to bring this mutation to people – to bring this new level of purity back to the Earth.

When *Dare to be Divine* was first conceived, I thought it would be too much. Our world is in a deep, dark phase of evolution. All around us are people who no longer believe in anything beyond death. We have forgotten our eternal roots. So, when I brought this wisdom out, I had no foundation to build it on. I hadn't written the Gene Keys book. Here I am fourteen years later, and Dare to be Divine still seems so fresh and bold to me...

THE 11TH SIDDHI – LIGHT
White Magick

I feel deeply drawn to the 11th Siddhi of Light. White magick always comes at the 11th hour! Pluto was actually in the 11th Gene Key when *Dare to be Divine* came through to me in 2004.

Pluto represents truth – hard-won Truth.

In essence, the Gene Keys are a system of higher white magick. They are a signature written in light. As you play with their transmission, the light comes into you and through you.

White magick is about working with higher beings. You must trust in the dreams the Divine has placed within you.

If they frighten you, those may be the most important ones! Ask your own truth barometer. Working with the pure light, ask for assistance. Not all higher beings can incarnate, for incarnation is a messy business. In some of them, the voltage is just too powerful, but they can still work through our auras.

Eden is a memory we all have access to. The 11th Gene Key is all about this memory of our body of light. Rather than join a group of monks in a monastery, we now have to bring the light into the medium of our everyday life in the world. The light of Eden combines both idealism and realism, and we have to span both poles.

THE 18TH SIDDHI — PERFECTION
The Perfect Paradox

The 18th Siddhi – Perfection. I adore this one. I am its greatest devotee. I am so imperfect that I just devote myself at the feet of this one. I take my shoes off before perfection. There are beings that have attained perfection. But we here in this world, we feel far from it. This is not a perfect world. Perfection is not possible here yet, although one day it will be.

In time the Earth will ascend into its own perfection. Time itself is the guarantee of it. Time is the road to perfection. This is why this whole transmission is about daring, because in an imperfect world, with imperfect people, to dare to be perfect is seen as insane. It seems to be the dream of an insane person!

But we are the dreamers. We will dream it into being, and every now and again, a higher being touches down and brings this reminder, like Ammaji.

Ammaji was born with the 17/18 axis. She is an avatar. The light works through her. She is known as the hugging saint. All she knows is how to give. There is nothing for her but to give.

This is what the light is and what it does. It thinks not about itself. That is the road to perfection and it alone will transform this planet.

AMMAJI

'It's all perfect' is a classic new age platitude, but the real test is: can you live that way in a crisis? Can you remember that when in great difficulty and suffering? It's all perfect, yes, but there is still so much to improve! That is the paradox.

So the question is: Is perfection an impossible dream? Perhaps not if enough high-frequency beings believe in it. Right now there are initiates incarnated all across the planet, more than there ever were before. Ask your truth barometer now, is this true?

A great synthesis is coming. It may take thousands of years to see it in the mass consciousness, but that's not our concern. Our concern is to build the foundation structure. One of the first things the field requires is to connect up the net of perfection through a sustained group vision. Then we place our trust in the noetic beings to guide each one of us, and then we watch the perfect symmetry unfold.

The plan is multi-generational. We will go on incarnating into this ideal, and as it builds, so the frequency builds. The driver is the 54th Siddhi – divine ambition.

In the I Ching the 18th hexagram is called *Work on what has been Spoilt*. It is here specifically to heal our minds. It is part of the Ring of Matter – four Gene Keys that govern the cycle of our childhood as we incarnate and come into the material world (57, 46, 48, 18).

This siddhi can heal our mental psychosis. We all suffer from psychosis in varying degrees. Because we are split in our brains, we are unable to see the world as it really is. The 18th Siddhi, therefore, heals mental illness. It can do that simply through the sacred geometry of its presence. In the presence of a divine mind, your mind begins to realign with the hologram of perfection. As you begin to taste and remember this perfection, your divided mind falls silent. This is how Christ threw out the demons. The presence of the 18th Siddhi, therefore, drives out our *collective* demons – all our inherited psychoses.

Something for all of us to contemplate.

THE 26TH SIDDHI – INVISIBILITY
The Earth Grid

We come now to the mystery known as the great cinnabar field...

The Earth is a grid of light, of invisible lines of force, like acupuncture meridians. These ley lines converge on places of power. Here in Britain one of these energy centres is called the 'Grail' – one of the great centres of the New Jerusalem. It was William Blake who uttered those famous lines: 'And did those feet in ancient times, walk upon England's mountains green?' The answer is yes, those feet did indeed come here.

New centres will appear around the world as the money begins to move towards the great vision. New temples will be built. These will not be the same kind of temples as in the past – temples used for worship. These will be practical temples – for the education of the future humans, with new eco-housing and new ways of doing things. This will occur in small ways at first, but then the movement will build more and more around the globe. Clairvoyants can already see the new temples along the grid lines of the great cinnabar field, just waiting to be built.

Here in Britain is a seat of enormous ancestral energy in the form of money. The USA was built out of this ancestral money. This is the energy bank. The 54th/53rd Gene Key programming partnership (in the Codon Ring of Seeking) concerns the correct transmutation of money.

In our body, the 26th Gene Key represents the thymus gland. It releases T-cells which clean the body by eradicating negativity. Globally, these cells are locations on the Earth's grid, and we operate collectively out of them. The ascension taking place through the Earth grid is happening everywhere. Initiates are being drawn to invisible forms as yet unbuilt.

The New World exists already on the lattice of these invisible dimensions. We need only visualise and bring it into form.

Dare to ascend!

THE 46TH SIDDHI – ECSTASY
Eating Mangoes

What is ecstasy? Here we can throw away all our concepts of failure and success. The spiritual teacher Osho once uttered the profound truth: 'Success has failed'. I love that one-liner!

Once you've been very successful in the material world, you begin to realise it has failed you. So you have to let go of 'more and more' and 'richer and richer' – and say to yourself, Okay, this hasn't worked. I have to do something else! and so you turn inwards. Inwards is the last place to go.

We have inherited many of our teachings from the East. We have to remember that. What we now need is a new teaching that is life-affirming, a teaching that celebrates life and the body and joy and laughter and dance. And sometimes foolery as well!

The 46th Gene Key reminds us that our body is the temple. So the real work is to build the New Jerusalem inside us.

The 46 is also a siddhi of serendipity, of good fortune. You just have to accept these truths of dare to be divine and your life will be transformed.

Master Omraam Mikael Aivanov one day made this great statement to the so-called realists. He said: 'Even if I am wrong, I prefer my delusion to your reality'.

OMRAAM MIKHAEL AIVANHOV

There is humour, delight, and fun to be had together. The revelation is not meant to be so serious. If you do the inner work, you will be discovered. The higher frequencies will reveal themselves to you through your thoughts, feelings, and dreams...

The 5th line of the 46th Gene Key is called *pronoia* – a wonderful word. It is the suspicion that the universe is out to help you. There's great humour in this 46.

This humour is well caught in Osho's figure of Zorba the Buddha. Enlightenment isn't all about buckets of water. Let's not forget why we're here. We're here for the ride. This is again what Osho taught. It's why he bought all those Rolls Royce's. Someone once asked him, How would you rather be enlightened? He said: In a Rolls Royce, of course! Whatever you may think of the man, he had a wicked sense of humour. As long as it doesn't hurt anyone, there's great fun to be had here on the material plane.

I lived for a year on the island of Maui in Hawaii. This is where the title 'eating mangoes' comes in. I had a heavenly time there. You could walk through the Maui forests – and still can, I am sure – and just pick up mangoes anywhere and eat them and the ecstasy from eating these mangoes is extraordinary. Anyway, there's this certain place on Maui called Kipahulu, and it's a dream of a place. It's a little slice of Eden where the energy is so exquisite. It's a place forgotten by time. There are places around the world like this, where Eden still persists.

So I was hanging out in a beautiful house there with this amazing garden seat. It was a beautiful, big wicker seat and I used to sit naked in this seat. It was so warm in Maui you could just sit anywhere naked. As I sat there day after day, I experienced the most exquisite forms of ecstasy as the warm, Pacific winds flowed across my naked body. I just felt what it was like to be innocent again, like a child – an eternal child.

That place is magical. Kipahulu. Even the sound of the word is ecstatic to me. So anyway, it's nice to share it with you. Don't tell too many people about it!

The Fifteenth Dare

THE SIXTEENTH DARE – DARE TO BE DIVINE

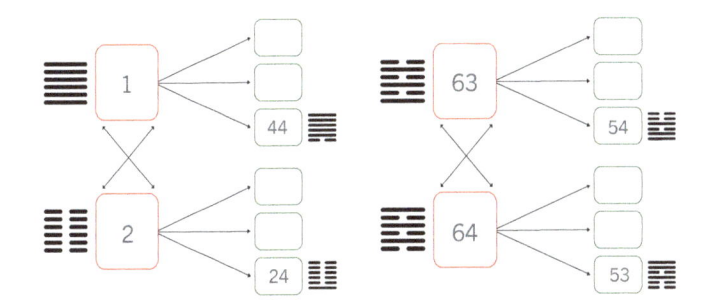

And so we come to our final dare. The 54 and the 53. Earth Ascending and the Pillar of Light. Is it not perfect our story ends with light?

THE 4 PILLARS OF THE TEMPLE

1 — FIRE
2 — WATER
63 — TRUTH
64 — LIGHT

We began with the sacred letters of light – the building blocks of our story. How can you tell a story without letters and words? So, we began with the understanding that all this is made up of these sacred letters, and these letters form these divine words – *Solve et coagula*, the secret of alchemy.

In part two we followed the descent of spirit into matter, the fall, and the birth of suffering.

In part three we explored the coming of *Homo sanctus*, the divine-human.

Finally in part four, the whole Earth, Gaia, also awakens to her higher nature. And as in any good fairy tale, we won't be able to truly understand many of the mysteries until we come towards the end.

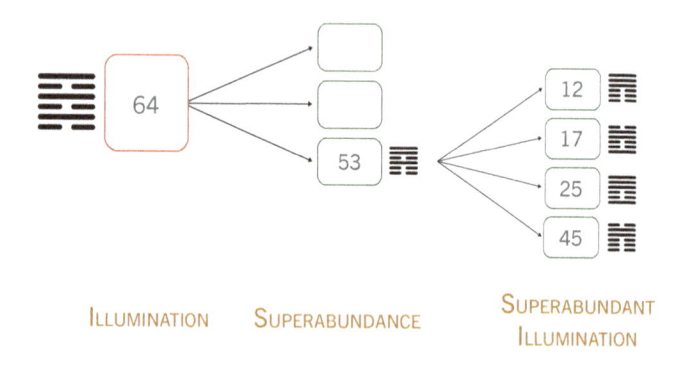

Illumination   Superabundance   Superabundant Illumination

THE 12 – **PURITY** – HEART OF A CHILD

THE 17 – **OMNISCIENCE** – THE EYE OF THE I

THE 25 – **UNIVERSAL LOVE** – THE GUILD OF THE GRAIL

THE 45 – **COMMUNION** – UNION OF ALL BEINGS

THE 12TH SIDDHI – PURITY

Heart of a Child

The 12th Siddhi has such beauty. It's about our innocent, pure heart.

This is the *puer eternis* – the eternal child of light – the one to whom the mysteries are revealed.

The thing with young children is their smell. Their purity has an aroma that cannot be copied. No clever technology could ever get near it! You can smell purity in a person.

There's even a strange esoteric word for it – *nyux*. I couldn't even find it on Google. Google isn't aware of it. But nyux is the word for the special transcendental aroma of a saint, of a pure one.

Each siddhi is a perfume distilled on the higher planes and then released onto the Earth plane. So the 12th Siddhi is about the huge wealth that lies in having an ideal. There's a deep secret here (this is the Ring of Secrets) in that the ideal has to be pure from the beginning.

Your ideal has to be selfless and collective. If you give in order to receive, it won't work. The greatest power ever is locked up in the ideal of heaven on Earth. Follow this ideal and all other things will be given to you. And this ideal is a living presence. Behind it lies this great fellowship of beings, these higher synarchies, and evolutions – the benevolent illuminati.

If you're working with this ideal of heaven on earth then you work with these higher beings. They will come into your aura. The ideal itself will go on sprouting through each of us. We each have to create our own branches of this new tree. Most of you already know your dreams, yet many of us lack the courage or the divine madness to believe in them. So, this great dream of the 12th Gene Key whispers to each of us:

Let go and abandon yourself to the ideal.

THE 17TH SIDDHI – OMNISCIENCE
The Eye of the I

Superabundance is about seeing the future and the past. It means to remember everything. It is to be omniscient.

In the end, we will remember it all. We will be able to replay all our lives and see the whole beautiful thread of our evolution. This is omniscience. All will be seen in its golden perfection.

I've told some of the stories about omniscience during this series. There are many of them. There are many great teachers who've displayed this siddhi. You know, it used to be much more common. In the Highlands of Scotland where I spent quite a bit of my youth, there was always a tradition of people with the sight, and it was often passed on genetically within the same family line.

Always in the world, there have been seers and oracles, but one day, we will all see through this single eye – this Eye of the I. And nothing is hidden from this eye. It's open right now. It sees you, it sees everything you do, everything you think, everything you say. It sees all.

The Eye opens towards the end of our evolution. It's a kind of finale. When this eye opens in humanity as a whole, illumination will pour through it and purify us.

With sight also comes the end of evil and corruption. That's why it's called the *evil eye* because it ends evil.

You cannot hide from yourself. You will have to face yourself. All those Divine eyes are staring into your being. They don't just stare. They cleanse you. This is the gaze of God.

Deunov, the great Bulgarian master one day said to his young pupil Aivanov: 'For you Mikael, a gaze is enough'.

Aivanov spent many years contemplating those words. Some people are so flammable, that all it takes is a tiny spark and they burst into the flames of Illumination.

Empty yourself of fear, worry, and concern. There are no real problems in this world. As we approach death we see this clearly again. The trick is to see it before we die, while in the midst of life. Then the Eye will stay open, and we will be free.

THE 25TH SIDDHI – UNIVERSAL LOVE
The Guild of the Grail

The 25 is the Guild of the Grail. This is universal love. And the Grail here is the ultimate symbol of endless wealth and superabundance. It is the everlasting cup. This is the principle around which all else revolves. This is the divine feminine, the hub of the Round Table – the ideal of Camelot. I love this myth because I live in this land. Ask someone else and they'll give you another myth.

According to divine law, the Grail is given only to those who already have. This is meant internally rather than externally. As in the New Testament parable of The Three Talents, you have to be proactive from your heart in order to receive. You cannot give because you want to receive. The 25th Siddhi is a cool love. It doesn't give to victims, but to those who can free victims.

Here is the nub. If you are closed off, if you are defended, if your heart has forgotten trust, if trauma has taken root so deeply in your cells that you cannot open, life cannot enter you and shower its blessings on you. Those in trauma need love above all else. They need unconditional, unending, patient love. Then the trauma will melt, the memory will soften over time, and once again love will enter.

Dare to be divine. Dare to open yourself to this love, in whatever form it comes to you in your life. The more advanced your spiritual evolution, the more your love will be tested...

In the end, nothing will fluster you or cause so much as a ripple in the ocean of your heart.

The Guild of the Grail is where we all come together to drink from the one cup – it is the universal love at the core that unites us. It is our source, the same in each of us so that as the forms dissolve away, the love is all that is left behind.

It is said that the Grail contains the blood of Christ. This is the blood of creation – the wine of love. When Jesus said, 'drink this in remembrance of me', he dared us to be divine. He confirmed that you and I are the same – we are one in this love. This was the 25th Siddhi speaking.

THE 45TH SIDDHI – COMMUNION
Union of all Beings

And so we reach the crest of the tsunami, the 45th Siddhi – a beautiful one to end on.

The sixteenth dare includes Purity, Omniscience, Love, and finally Communion. You see how the pattern flows from one siddhi into another...

Superabundance is life itself. The 45th Siddhi is in the Ring of Prosperity and unifies all beings, all hierarchies. We have already seen how synarchy contains hierarchy within itself. In this way, everything is ordered to perfection, and in this great order – *the last shall be first.*

This means that the closer you come to the centre, the greater is the flow of light through the eye of the divine heart. Then the light is refracted through the shards and prisms of all the divine forms. This is why in Tibetan sacred paintings, for example, you see Avalokiteshwara, a dancing deity filled with eyes. Those eyes are all the multifarious forms – lives through which the divine light plays and each of us is one of those eyes.

And as this 45th Siddhi dawns in humanity, we will turn our eyes to our children, to those more innocent than ourselves in the web of life. Our children are also the animals, plants, and the beautiful beings we share our planet with. Just as the angels look upon us with that limitless compassion and love, so will we look upon those below us. They are not in fact 'below' us, but that is the limitation of language.

True governance, which is the essence of the 45th Siddhi, is compassion. The natural order of life is expressed through pure-hearted beings. This is the pure life. And the Grail at the hub is the divine ideal around which all beings revolve. This is the web of all beings. This is the Round Table I have been talking about. Another mystic name for it is the *antahkarana*.

Thus will we rebuild our world by looking and seeing through the eyes of our children, and we will never harm anyone or anything. That will be our creed. We won't kill for any reason. How can you kill as a child? This is where we're headed as a species. Dare to be divine means that we all come together, we all gather together. That's the name of this hexagram – *Gathering Together*. We work together in harmony. We are a symphony of beings, and the bliss that will come from the music we will make is beyond our wildest imaginings. What else can I say? Dare to be divine.

Place yourself in service to those who most need your help. Offer them your love and invite them to the communion table. Do this in the name of love and communion. And all you ever dreamed of will come to be.

Thank you for journeying with me during these teachings.

May your life be blessed.

IMAGE ACKNOWLEDGEMENTS

Zarathustra – page 35, Nicholas Roerich (1931), Public Domain

Ramana Maharshi – page 44, Photographer: G.G. Welling (1948)

The Storm on the Sea of Galilee – page 53, Rembrandt (1633), Public Domain

Yogananda – page 54, Public Domain

Meher Baba – page 60, © 2003-2010 The Avata Meher Baba Perpetual Public Charitable Trust, Ahmednagar, India

Sathya Sai Baba – page 72, CC BY-SA 4.0, Photo:©Guy Veloso (1996)

Peter Deunov – page 81, Petardanov.com (1996)

Babi Hari Dass – page 88, CC BY-SA 4.0, Photo:©Pradeepwb (2006)

Bawa Muhaiyaddeen – page 108, CC BY-SA 3.0

Sri Sai Baba of Shirdi – page 119, licensed under CC BY 2.0; Bhakua

Drukpa Kunley – page 140, b. 1455 – d.1529, Artist Unkown

Neem Karoli Baba – page 147, Author: Prabhard

Sri Yukteswar – page 158, Free Public Domain, Paramahansa Yogananda. Autobiography of a Yogi. (New York: Philosophical Library, 1946)

Sri Aurobindo – *page 186*, Sri Aurobindo Ashram Trust (c 1900)

Auroville – *page 187*, CC PDM 1.0 by ljsajonia

Ammaji – *page 202*, Audebaud, Jean Louis (JLA974), CC BY 2.0 via Wikimedia Commons

Omraam Mikhael Aivanhov – *page 205*, Used by permission (Sonne17)

Other Books by Richard Rudd

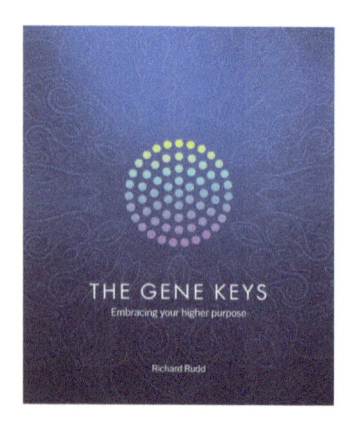

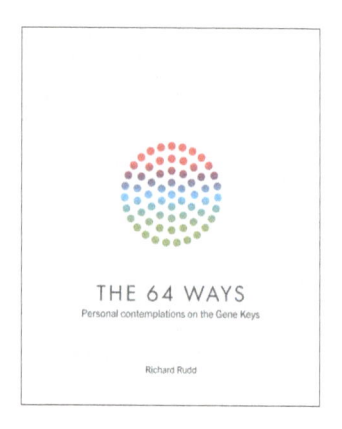

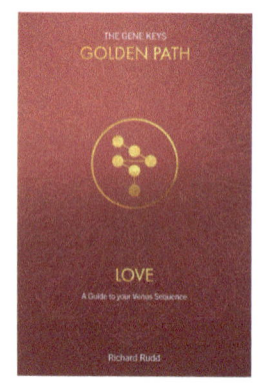

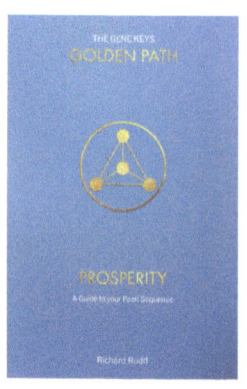

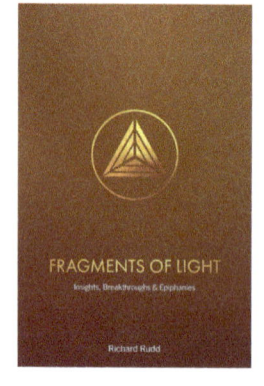

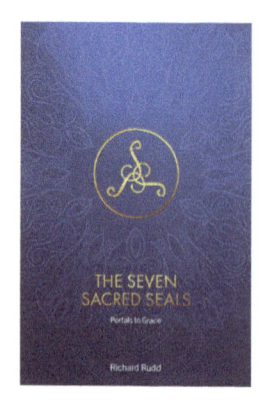

The Gene Keys
Embracing your higher purpose
Richard Rudd

The 64 Ways
Personal contemplations on the Gene Keys
Richard Rudd

The Gene Keys Golden Path — Genius
A Guide to your Activation Sequence
Richard Rudd

The Gene Keys Golden Path — Love
A Guide to your Venus Sequence
Richard Rudd

The Gene Keys Golden Path — Prosperity
A Guide to your Pearl Sequence
Richard Rudd

The Gene Keys Golden Path — Harmony
A Guide to your Star Pearl
Richard Rudd

Fragments of Light
Insights, Breakthroughs & Epiphanies
Richard Rudd

The Seven Sacred Seals
Portals to Grace
Richard Rudd

genekeys.com/books

Other Books by Richard Rudd

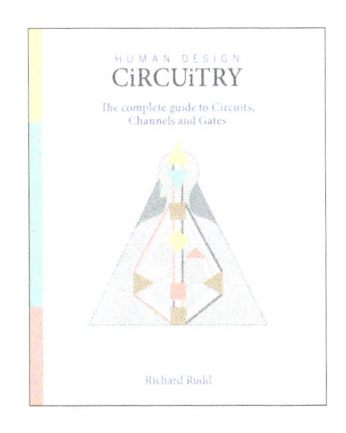

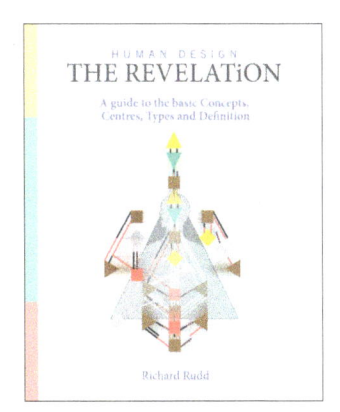

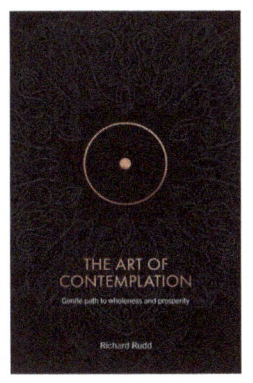

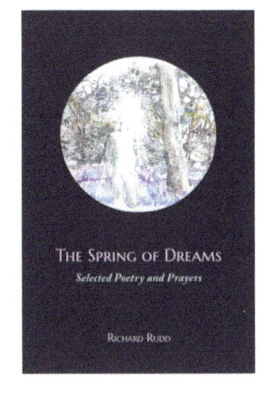

genekeys.com/books

Milton Keynes UK
Ingram Content Group UK Ltd.
UKHW020852060923
428102UK00002B/26